M000268239

WHAT PEOPLE ARE SAYING ABOUT *PUTTING ON MANHOOD*:

"I just finished reading *Putting On Manhood* and can tell you I really enjoyed it. Thank you for sharing this challenge to men to become more like Christ by becoming the men of God HE has called us to be. *Putting On Manhood* is a direct yet engaging challenge to men as disciples of Christ to live out the reality of what it means to follow Jesus. I recommend this book to every man who is serious about his relationship to the Lord. Christianity is not about where we go and what we do Sunday morning but how we live our lives. This practical volume gets to the everyday issues men face in their family relationships, work environment, and personal challenges through Jamie's personal experience and biblical training in the things of God." —**Dr. Stephen R. Tourville**, *PennDel Ministry Network Superintendent.*

"I was blessed, challenged, and encouraged as I read this book. In every man's life there are many seasons, circumstances, tests, and trials that try to strip us of our God-given armor. This book is a reminder to the men of America to put on manhood!" —**Brian Pruitt**, *Founder & CEO, Power of Dad Ministries.*

"In *Putting On Manhood*, Jamie Holden writes as he lives, with an openness, transparency, and commitment to see men stand up and put on Manhood! Jamie's stories are real and down to earth. He brings each principle he teaches to life and ends each chapter with thought-provoking questions. *Putting On Manhood* will help you and your 'band of brothers' pull out the weeds of your past and live a life that is worthy of your calling!" —**Tom Rees**, *HonorBound Men's Director, PennDel Ministry Network.*

"A tremendous resource for men or your men's group! After reading it, you come away with an understanding of the passion Jamie has for men's ministry and the importance of the Mantour. A glimpse into a man's world, the struggles and victories of being a godly man, with a great workbook to share with a small group of men trying to walk the walk." —**Thomas J. Sember**, *Conference Speaker & former New York District Men's Ministry Director.*

PUTTING ON

MANHOOD

THE COURAGEOUS JOURNEY TO BIBLICAL MATURITY

JAMES J. HOLDEN

Published by 4One Ministries, Inc.

Previously Published by Morning Joy Media.

Design: Debbie Capeci

Cataloging-In-Publication Data

Subject Headings:

  1. Christian life 2. Men's Issues 3. Spiritual formation.

ISBN 978-0-9988492-9-4

Printed in the United States of America

This book is dedicated to three men who have been examples to me over the years of what it means to put on manhood and live as a godly man. Thank you Tom Sember, Tom Rees, and Daniel McNaughton for investing in me, challenging me, and believing in me. I appreciate you all for your friendship and support!

I also dedicate it to two very special ladies:

My mother, Kathy Holden, who invested her entire life into supporting me and raising me to follow God. I miss you and I hope you would be proud of the man I have grown up to be.

My big sister and best friend, Adessa Holden. Thank you for your constant support. I couldn't have asked for a better sister to grow up with. I appreciate you so much and look forward to all the adventures God still has for us!

Finally, I thank my father, Jim Holden, for allowing me to share my full testimony in order to help other men avoid the same mistakes and pitfalls both he and I have made in our lives. I appreciate your willingness to share your part of our story!

CONTENTS

INTRODUCTION

When I was a child, I talked like a child, I thought like a child, I reasoned like a child. When I became a man, I put the ways of childhood behind me.

I Corinthians 13:11

I firmly believe God is doing a new and mighty work in the hearts of men. The theme God is speaking to me over and over is that it's time for men to stand up and put on manhood.

The word God has given me to share with men today is that he isn't looking for followers who are staying stuck in their childish ways. He is looking for men! He is seeking men who will lay aside their childish ways, whether it be addictions, struggles, generational iniquities, sins, or attitudes. God is looking for his men to stand up and say "I am putting on manhood!"

Every man will have to make this decision at some point in his life. I know I did. I grew up with a mom who modeled to me daily what it means to serve God wholeheartedly. My mom loved God with everything inside of her, and she raised my sister and me to follow God and serve him with total abandon. My dad was the exact opposite.

Shortly after my mom got saved, my dad began attending church with her. He went up for an altar call and accepted Jesus into his life. But he never put aside his childish ways. He never changed and became a different man. He just said a sinner's prayer and kept living the same way.

My dad went to church every week. He became a respected man in the church, eventually becoming a board member and elder. But he wasn't serving God. He was going through the motions. In the privacy of his own home, he was an abuser. He was a master manipulator. He was a diagnosed pathological liar. He was not what everyone thought him to be.

I grew up in this situation, with a mom who was devoted to God and a dad everyone called a godly man. As many young boys do, I idolized my dad. He could do no wrong in my eyes. Sure, emotionally he abused me, controlled me, and a few times, hit me. But hey, I deserved it; it was my fault. That's what I thought. Admiring him the way I did, I slowly grew up to be just like him.

When I was twenty, our lives exploded. Through a series of events, I came to find out my dad was living a double life. He had secrets. He had another life. He was not who everyone thought he was.

I was devastated. I quickly went from a boy who idolized his dad to a man who despised his father. I *hated* him with everything inside of me. The only thing was **I had become just like him**.

I was a liar. I was abusive. I was controlling and a manipulator. I was domineering and degraded women. I was addicted to porn. I was following down the same road my dad went on.

Most of all, I was breaking my mother's heart. She prayed for me daily to turn myself around and get back in line with God. She begged God to open my eyes. She tried to point out to me how much I was like my dad, and how I needed to change. But I didn't listen to her. I couldn't see what she was telling me. After all, I was a Bible college graduate. I had a call on my life to minister and serve. Who did she think she was to tell me these things?

Eventually though, God answered her prayers, and he showed me exactly who I had become. Through a series of events in which I totally lost control in a violent rage, I came to see I needed help. The details of that night are described in a later chapter. When my eyes were opened to my awful behavior, I was devastated by my actions. Instantly, I felt like God could never use me again since I was capable of this kind of behavior. I cried for hours. I felt hopeless and ashamed.

I cried out to God for help. I surrendered myself to his control. I begged him to help me overcome my childish ways and become a man of God. I confessed to him that I had no idea what it meant to be a godly man. I knew how to be a hypocrite. I knew how to be an abuser. I knew how to be oppressive. But when it came to being godly, I was clueless.

I'm thankful God heard my cries, and over the next few years, he did a deep work inside me. He began transforming me into a new man. He showed me how to put on godly manhood. Throughout the rest of this book, we will be discussing putting on manhood as I share the same principles God taught me.

Where did this theme of this book, *putting on manhood*, come from? Recently I was talking with a friend who told me how discouraged he had become with the men's ministry in his area of the country. Morale among the men was low. Turnout was even lower. Men just weren't connecting and growing in their walk with God.

As he spoke, I understood what he was saying. I had also been going through a period of time where I was wrestling with how to get men more interested in our ministry. I honestly felt like my ministry was failing, but as I talked with this man, I came to see it wasn't my ministry; it was men's ministry as a whole.

Later, another friend told me how discouraged he was at the lack of turnout at a men's event he had planned. Even more discouraging was the fact that *no one*, not one man, responded to the message during the altar call.

Then a few weeks later, we participated in a big men's convention. As men came up to our display and spoke, I began to sense the same feelings of frustration from them that I had been feeling and my friends had shared. Men were down and discouraged. Their church's men's ministries were floundering. Many had come to the convention alone because they couldn't get a group of men together to come with them.

As I drove home from the convention, I asked God what was going on. What was wrong with the men in his church? Where was the disconnect? More importantly, what was the answer?

I got home, had dinner, and as is often the case after a convention, I was absolutely exhausted, so I went to bed. However, sleep was on my agenda, not God's.

As I lay in bed struggling to sleep, God began stirring within me this message of *putting on manhood*. He reminded me of a statistic I often quote: **four out of every ten men had no father living in their home when they were growing up**. This doesn't even include those who had dads in the home who were abusive, absent, or workaholics. Then, God showed me the era of fatherlessness that has come to roost in America. We have churches filled with men who are saved, want to serve God, and want to be godly men. Yet men's ministry is dying, groups are shrinking, and spiritual apathy is taking over our men. Why? Men are stuck in their childish patterns. They aren't putting on manhood.

Men say they have no time to pray and read the Bible. They are just too busy in our fast-paced world, yet these same men somehow find time to run their fantasy football teams and keep up with the latest in television, movies, and electronics. I am not talking about teenagers; I am talking about grown men, men who haven't put away childish things. However, **I don't blame these men**.

No one taught them. No one showed them the value of hard work. No man instilled in them the concept of enjoying hobbies like home repair, car repair, or gardening, activities that are productive and beneficial. They were raised by parents who used video games and TV as babysitters while they tried to meet their own needs inside. But God wants to do something new!

Men across the country are waiting for God to do something. I believe God is waiting for men to do something! Let me give you an example.

I want to get into better shape, get fit, and lose some weight. After asking God how to do it, he miraculously provided me with a Bowflex machine to use in my home, a brand-new machine for free! However, if I don't take action and actually use the machine, it does me no good.

God wants to raise up men who are godly men. He wants men committed to him, to his ways, and to developing relationships. It is time men put away childish things. It is time to hang it up, get in the game, and become God's man!

We need to start applying the lesson Paul teaches us in 1 Corinthians 13:11:

> *When I was a child, I talked like a child, I thought like a child, I reasoned like a child. When I became a man, I put the ways of childhood behind me.*

We need to put our childish things, our old way of thinking and acting, our natural mindset, behind us, and we need to put on manhood. In this book, we are going to learn just how to do that.

Men across the country are waiting for God to do something. I believe God is waiting for *men* to do something!

We're going to start by looking at the need to stop letting ourselves get so easily entangled in childish things and to start running the race set before us. Then we are going to dive into how to put on manhood. We're going to discuss:

- Following God wholeheartedly
- Prioritizing our lives
- Being devoted to God
- Being accountable
- Forgiving
- Living a Spirit-filled life

In the final section, we'll learn how to be men who live a life worthy of the calling. We will discuss what this phrase means, and discover how we apply it to our lives. We will learn:

- How to be financially responsible
- How to act like men with women
- The importance of obedience
- How to serve others
- How to sacrifice

That is the vision. The goal is to put away childish things and to put on manhood. We can do it together. We can grow in our walk with God, our families, and our relationships with others. We can stop letting Satan kick our butts, and we can start doing some butt-kicking of our own. Let's get started!

NOTE: *To make things easier for all readers, we put the group study questions at the end of each chapter for men to review on their own. For the convenience of those using the book in a small group, we have also included the study questions in the workbook section so you don't have to flip back and forth between chapters.*

SECTION I

WHAT ARE WE TO TAKE OFF?

·1·

SCRUBBING UP BEFORE WE GET DRESSED

Imagine the following situation. It's a beautiful, sunny Saturday. You've been working in your yard all day. You spent a good part of the morning on your hands and knees pulling weeds. Then you pushed your lawn mower back and forth across your lawn, leaving it trimmed and pristine. You grab some lunch, then right back to work, spreading fertilizer on your wife's flower beds so they grow beautiful and strong. You wrap up the yard work marathon by spraying some pesticide around your garden.

Your yard work is complete, and you are just beautiful to behold! Your hands and arms are covered in dirt. Bits of the fertilizer are under your fingernails. Your shirt is drenched with sweat, and it is not exactly a scent of fine roses floating out from under your armpits. Hey, you earned that smell through lots of hard work!

You walk in the house, and your family takes one look at you and bursts out laughing at how dirty you are. You tease them by chasing your kids and threatening to hug them, and they run away laughing. Your wife tells you, "Honey, you need to get moving, we are meeting our friends for dinner in an hour. You better start getting ready."

Now, how many of you would go to your bedroom, get undressed, and immediately put on your nice, go-to-dinner clothes? No one would do this! We would never put our dirty bodies into our clean clothes! We would hop in the shower, get all cleaned up and smelling nice, and then get dressed.

How many of us do this in our spiritual lives, though? How often do people get saved, and then continue on the same way as before accepting Christ as Savior? We don't stop and look at the things that keep us in our childish ways and prevent us from putting on manhood. We all need to take a hard look at ourselves and start looking at the things that keep us from growing in our walk with God.

Hebrews 12:1 sums it up best:

Therefore, since we are surrounded by such a great cloud of witnesses, let us throw off everything that hinders and the sin that so easily entangles. And let us run with perseverance the race marked out for us.

This verse tells us we need to throw off everything that hinders us. We need to chuck off all the sins that keep us from being able to put on manhood. We need to see the childish things we're still doing and the childish thought patterns that prevent us from spiritually maturing. One of the biggest traps entangling men today are stereotypes.

Stereotypes? How can stereotypes entangle us? It's very easy. When we fall prey to the stereotypes of what a *real man* is according to the world, we are not allowing the Holy Spirit to make us into what *he wants* us to be. Instead, we are letting the world define us. Think about some of the stereotypes the world places on men:

- Men hate to read.
- Men look at other women. Wives just have to get used to it; men can't help it.
- Men can't stay pure. Our natural tendency is to conquer women, so how can we be expected to be with only one woman for our entire lives?

- Men don't have time to pray or read the Bible. Our society is too fast paced and we have too much to do.
- Men don't talk. We are strong and silent. We don't need to discuss our every thought and feeling.
- Men aren't emotional. We don't cry or get emotionally involved.

These are just a few of the many lies our culture has convinced us are true of men. God's men are buying into the world's stereotypes. They are not putting on manhood because they're too busy wearing the clothes the world lays out for them.

Recently, our women's ministry division, A Well-Rounded Woman Ministries, received a letter from a man who offered to write an article to help women better understand men. My sister, Adessa, who runs the women's ministry, graciously agreed to read his article, making no promises she would use it.

When the man sent her the article, she read it and immediately forwarded it to me. This Christian man had done what he said he would do—write an article explaining men to women. Unfortunately, his view of men was the world's view, not God's view.

His article contained such pearls of wisdom as "Women should take their spouses on a trip to a well-known lingerie store and put on a show for them, but not be offended if their man looks at other women there too, because men can't help it." He said, "Hey, my wife isn't the young beauty I had married," and he looks at other women, but it doesn't mean he doesn't love his wife.

He also gave advice on communicating. He suggested women need to realize they have to stop trying to discuss things with their husbands, because their husbands don't care and don't want to have emotional discussions. They shouldn't try and discuss their relationships; they just need to keep it to themselves and get over it.

He mentioned that women shouldn't expect their husbands to cry, and if he ever did cry, rush him to the hospital immediately, because he must be dying! These are just a sampling of his words of wisdom about what women need to know about men. The entire article was one stereo-type after another that excused men for everything they do and placed all responsibility for any issues on the wife. It never mentioned the need for men to grow and change and pursue godliness. It was just one example after another of "this is just how all men are, get used to it"!

Needless to say, the article made a quick appearance in my computer's recycle bin. You know the saddest part? The man who wrote the article was a pastor!

Though this man was from another part of the country and unknown to me, as a pastor he was called to speak God's truth to the world, but instead he had bought into the world's stereotypes and opinions of men. Instead of encouraging men to grow and change and become all they could in God, he encouraged them to stay as they were, because it was just natural.

After reading his article, my first thoughts were anger at what he was teaching men. But the more I thought about it, the more it broke my heart. Why? Because, while the article showed his wrong view on manhood, the article wasn't written for men. It was written for women. The goal of the article was to bind God's precious daughters in chains to men and tell them *they* were the reason for issues in their marriage. They were the ones who didn't understand. They were the ones who had to change and accept ungodly behavior from their men. My heart broke at the thought of what a grief-stricken woman would get for counseling if she turned to this pastor for support after hearing of her husband's affair, or her husband's abusiveness and control over her and her children—all because of a man in authority buying into stereotypes.

I don't share this story to judge this man. I share it to show how ste-reotypes are infiltrating the church. The world's ways of looking at men are becoming the church's way of thinking.

Sex before marriage is no longer being criticized. After all, men can't be expected to stay pure until they get married. Pornography is being excused as man's weakness instead of encouraging men to stand up, resist, and conquer the temptation.

Developing a strong spiritual walk is downplayed because men can't possibly find time for prayer and Bible reading. Sure, they can rattle off all the stats from their favorite sports team, and they can describe in detail all the action sequences in the latest action flick, but we can't expect them to have time to spend with God.

These are just a few examples of how we are being deceived. The media tells a man of God he can't have convictions and morals. For example, he can't call homosexuality or abortion a sin; he has to be more tolerant.

Hollywood tells us we can't be good fathers or dads. After all, the few TV shows that actually have a father in the setting portray him as a dunce whose wife runs the household. Almost every episode portrays the husband caving in on any convictions or morals he may have.

> **God's men are buying into these stereotypes and we are staying in our childish ways.**

However, even this is rare to find, since most TV shows are no longer set around family life. Instead, they show single people who spend their time sleeping around and drinking. Instead of encouraging men to settle down, marry, and raise a family, they encourage men to work, keep all his money for his enjoyment, stay unattached, and sleep with a different woman every day. As soon as a woman looks for a commitment, cut all ties and move on to the next one-night stand. Instead of pushing a committed marriage relationship, Hollywood pushes friends with benefits.

The appalling thing is that God's children are buying into these stereotypes, and we are staying in our childish ways. My brothers, this should not be!

Society should not be our gauge; the Word of God is our standard. We get our convictions and morals from the Bible. If we are to successfully put on manhood, we have to get rid of the stereotypes that keep us bound to childish ways.

Let's look again at our sample list of stereotypes and see what the Bible teaches us about them:

Stereotype: Men don't read to learn and grow.
Truth: We need to read and study God's Word.

Study to shew thyself approved unto God, a workman that needeth not to be ashamed, rightly dividing the word of truth (2 Timothy 2:15 KJV).

Keep this Book of the Law always on your lips; meditate on it day and night, so that you may be careful to do everything written in it. Then you will be prosperous and successful (Joshua 1:8).

All Scripture is God-breathed and is useful for teaching, rebuking, correcting and training in righteousness, so that the servant of God may be thoroughly equipped for every good work (2 Timothy 3:16–17).

Stereotype: Men look at women; wives just have to get used to it. Men can't help it.
Truth: Men can control their eyes and what they look at.

I made a covenant with my eyes not to look lustfully at a young woman (Job 31:1).

You have heard that it was said, 'You shall not commit adultery.' But I tell you that anyone who looks at a woman lustfully has already committed adultery with her in his heart. If your right eye causes you to stumble, gouge it out and throw it away. It is better for you to lose one part of your body than for your whole body to be thrown into hell (Matthew 5:27–29).

Stereotype: Men can't stay pure. Our natural tendency is to conquer women, so how can we be expected to be with only one woman at a time?

Truth: God created marriage in the Garden of Eden, and designed it to be a monogamous lifetime commitment.

Give honor to marriage, and remain faithful to one another in marriage. God will surely judge people who are immoral and those who commit adultery (Hebrews 13:4 NLT).

Sex is as much spiritual mystery as physical fact. As written in Scripture, "The two become one." Since we want to become spiritually one with the Master, we must not pursue the kind of sex that avoids commitment and intimacy, leaving us lonelier than ever—the kind of sex that can never "become one" (1 Corinthians 6:16 The Message).

Stereotype: Men don't have time to pray or read the Bible. Our society is too fast paced and we have too much to do.

Truth: We find time for the things that are a priority.

But seek first his [God's] kingdom and his righteousness, and all these things will be given to you as well (Matthew 6:33).

Stereotype: Men aren't emotional. We don't cry or get emotionally involved.

Truth: Real men have emotions—that's the way God created us.

When Jesus saw her weeping, and the Jews who had come along with her also weeping, he was deeply moved in spirit and troubled.
 "Where have you laid him?" he asked.
 "Come and see, Lord," they replied.
 Jesus wept (John 11:33–35).

And when He came near the gate of the city, behold, a dead man was being carried out, the only son of his mother; and she was a widow. And a large crowd from the city was with her. When the Lord saw her, He had compassion on her... (Luke 7:12–13 NKJV).

This is just a brief sample of how the Bible totally contradicts the world's stereotypes of men. If there is such a stark contrast, then why do men still believe the world's lies?

> **The enemy is deceiving God's men to keep them bound to their childish ways. He knows the potential God's sons have when they put on manhood, so he tries to keep them bound in the ways of the world.**

The reason is simple. Men are being deceived. The enemy is deceiving them to keep them bound to their childish ways. He knows the potential God's sons have when we put on manhood, so he tries to keep us bound in the ways of the world. That's why we need to obey Hebrews 12:1: *Therefore, since we are surrounded by such a great cloud of witnesses, let us throw off everything that hinders and the sin that so easily entangles. And let us run with perseverance the race marked out for us.*

We have to throw it off and run toward godly manhood. I love the first part of that verse. We are surrounded by a great cloud of witnesses. The Bible is full of men who threw off their childish ways. Men like Joshua, David, Peter, and Paul are shining examples for us. They did it, and so can we.

We can put away our childish ways and the things that entangle us, and we can run toward manhood. God is calling men from around the world to become a new cloud of witnesses to this generation, men who are leaving their old lives behind, men who are abandoning the ways of the world and pursuing the ways of God. Will you accept this call to put away childish things and put on manhood? If so, let's continue on together!

24

GROUP STUDY QUESTIONS

1. What are some of the things that entangle you and keep you from growing in your walk with God?

2. What steps can you take to break free from these entanglements?

3. How can we as a group help you?

4. We listed some of the stereotypes men face. What are some additional stereotypes?

5. What stereotype affects you the most?

6. Are you committed to the journey of putting on manhood?

SECTION II

PUTTING ON MANHOOD

·2·

HOW FAR ARE YOU WILLING TO GO?

I shall be telling this with a sigh
Somewhere ages and ages hence:
Two roads diverged in a wood, and I—
I took the one less traveled by,
And that has made all the difference.

These famous lines by Robert Frost are the perfect description of where many of us find ourselves in our walk with God. You see, many men have decided to take the more common road, the road that keeps them living in their childish ways. However, there is another road awaiting us all, the road to manhood, the road less traveled. The man who chooses this road won't always find it to be an easy trail, but trust me: it is the best trail to choose.

We all need to decide what road we will choose. We always have the option of staying in our childish ways. However, if you want more from life, you need to put on manhood.

The first question we need to ask ourselves when we decide to put on manhood is, just how far are we willing to go? Are we willing to cast anything and everything aside to become the man God wants us to be?

Of course we are! We all rise up and say we will do whatever we need to do serve God. But will we really?

The people of Israel faced a similar choice thousands of years ago. Their glorious leader Joshua, one of my favorite men in the entire Bible, was old and preparing to die. He had led the people of Israel in amazing campaigns of war, and they had made great strides in obtaining the blessings God had for them. However, Joshua was about to die, and he wouldn't be there to lead them. They had a decision to make. Let's look at Joshua 24:1: *Then Joshua gathered all the tribes of Israel to Shechem and called for the elders of Israel, for their heads, for their judges, and for their officers; and they presented themselves before God* (NKJV).

Joshua had a particular message for the nation of Israel. For years, he had valiantly led the nation on one of the greatest military conquests ever known to man. He courageously guided the people to victory against every enemy they encountered. Now the nation of Israel was free to dwell in the beauty of their Promised Land. It seemed Joshua's work was done. He led them to victory. He defeated their enemies. All that was left to do was to leave a legacy for the nation.

For the sake of time, allow me to summarize the message. (You may want to take a moment and read Joshua 24:1–13.)

Joshua begins his message with a recap of all that God had done over the years for the people of Israel. Beginning with Abraham, he retells how God had chosen Israel as his own people. He relates how the people went into slavery in Egypt and how God had given them freedom. He continues to remind them of the many ways God had protected them and kept them safe from their enemies on the way to the Promised Land. He makes it clear to them that God was the one responsible for the freedom and blessings they currently enjoyed.

They had done nothing to deserve it. He did it all. It was a beautiful reminder of the grace and love of God to the nation of Israel.

Once Joshua laid the groundwork of his speech with this walk down memory lane, he goes immediately into the heart of his message. Joshua gives them the alternatives. Let's look at Joshua 24 (NKJV), beginning at verse 15:

Alternative Number One:

And if it seems evil to you to serve the LORD, choose for yourselves this day whom you will serve, whether the gods which your fathers served that were on the other side of the River.

The first alternative Joshua presented to the Israelites was the gods of their fathers. Many years earlier, the nation of Israel began worshipping other gods. They adopted the gods of the Egyptians while living in slavery. Once free, they began to serve the gods of the desert nations in which they wandered. While these gods had done nothing to help the children of Israel gain victory over their enemies, Joshua wanted to give them the option of choosing their fathers' way of life. We have the same option.

We all know many of the generational sins and iniquities of our ancestors. We have the option of ignoring these patterns and to continue practicing them. Granted, they won't bring us to our Promised Land, but it's an option nonetheless. Joshua makes it clear that if serving God isn't desirable, then we can choose our fathers' ways. However, this isn't the only alternative he offers.

Alternative Number Two:

And if it seems evil to you to serve the Lord, choose for yourselves this day whom you will serve…or the gods of the Amorites, in whose land you dwell.

The second alternative to serving the Lord was to serve the gods of the culture in which they now lived. The surrounding nations had lots of gods they could choose to follow. They could serve Baal. They could build their Ashtoreth poles. They could go to the temples of the prostitutes. No one was forcing them to serve God because of all that he had done for them. They were free to choose. We have this same freedom.

There are lots of gods in our culture we can choose to serve. We can serve the stereotypes we discussed in the last chapter. We can serve the god of power. We can dedicate our lives to the god of success. The god of play is a choice many people enjoy serving. Sensual pleasure can be our god of choice.

Our world is surrounded by millions of gods which can take the place of serving God. These gods are one way we stay stuck in our childish ways. We have the option to choose these gods; however, they come with a price. Joshua knew the price and made his choice.

Serving the Lord

>...*But as for me and my house, we will serve the* LORD.

Joshua had no doubt in his mind which God he would serve. He chose to serve the Lord. Joshua threw down a gauntlet for the people to choose. There was no doubt in his mind what his choice would be, but he wanted the people to choose for themselves. As we read on, we see that their response was immediate...a little too immediately for Joshua's taste.

> *So the people answered and said: "Far be it from us that we should forsake the* LORD *to serve other gods; for the* LORD *our God is He who brought us and our fathers up out of the land of Egypt, from the house of bondage, who did those great signs in our sight, and preserved us in all the way that we went and among all the people through whom we passed. And the* LORD *drove out from before us all the people, including the Amorites who dwelt in the land. We also will serve the* LORD, *for He is our God."*

But Joshua said to the people, "You cannot serve the LORD, for He is a holy God. He is a jealous God; He will not forgive your transgressions nor your sins. If you forsake the Lord and serve foreign gods, then He will turn and do you harm and consume you, after He has done you good."

It's easy to make a promise in the heat of the moment, but in the end you must keep your promise. Joshua knew that the people hadn't counted the cost. They hadn't thought it through.

They didn't consider the hard work necessary to serve God wholeheartedly. Their natural disposition was not to submit to God. It would take hard work to retrain themselves to keep their word. He knew they hadn't thought about the consequences of breaking their vow. He tells his concerns to the people. He then waits for their answer.

> **It's easy to make promises in the heat of the moment, but in the end you must keep your promise. So count the cost!**

And the people said to Joshua, "No, but we will serve the LORD!" So Joshua said to the people, "You are witnesses against yourselves that you have chosen the LORD for yourselves, to serve Him." And they said, "We are witnesses!"

The choice is made. They decided they will serve the Lord. Joshua accepts their answer. Then, he teaches them how to keep their word.

"Now therefore," he said, "put away the foreign gods which are among you, and incline your heart to the LORD God of Israel."

The only way they could serve the Lord was to remove all the sin in their lives. They had to put their childish ways behind them and put on manhood. They had to choose to serve only God. Anything else needed to go. The same is true for us.

We need to make the decision to put aside our childish things and pursue God wholeheartedly. We can't let anything keep us from developing a heart that places no limits on how far we will go with God.

We need to make developing a personal walk with God our top priority. God doesn't just want men who say they are Christians; he wants men who are wholeheartedly devoted to him.

We all need to ask ourselves, how far will we go for God? Will we go part way, or will we be totally abandoned and surrendered to him?

The Christian walk is hard. It isn't always candy canes and gumdrops… but there is no better road to be on than the road to godly manhood! The question is, will you travel it?

Deciding how far to go for God is an issue we all must face. In order to reach our full potential as God's man, we must be willing to hold nothing back.

This is a decision I have had to face. Even with all the garbage in my life I described to you earlier, I always had a heart for God. I wanted to follow and serve him. However, I was not one hundred percent sold out. My heart was divided.

Because of my many physical problems and the abuse in my past, I never felt I was a real man. I was always pursuing things to help me feel like one. I desired a fancy car, high-tech electronic equipment, and a successful career. I obsessively followed sports, and video games ruled my free time. I wanted a huge ministry and the approval of others. My relationship with God shared time with these other interests, and usually God got the leftovers.

God began to show me that my heart was divided. He wanted me facing and dealing with my manhood issues, not running from them and burying myself in other things. I had to make a decision: was I going to continue allowing my heart to be divided, or follow God wholeheartedly?

I chose to leave the other things, let God work inside of me, and follow him. I no longer have to prove I am a real man because I know I have become a godly man.

Multiple times God has asked me how far I am willing to go for him. Was I willing to give up my hopes and desires to follow God into a place of waiting as he healed the past pain of hurt and abuse? Would I lay down my financial security and trust God to supply my needs as I moved into the free-will offering ministry he called me to do? Would I involve myself in a community that had zero benefit to me, but in which I could benefit other people? Countless times God has challenged me to give up my desires, surrender them to him, and allow him to do what he wants me to do.

I have had to give up dreams, aspirations, relationships, thought patterns, and even the image I tried to present to people in order to wholeheartedly follow God. He didn't let me keep anything that kept me from wholeheartedly following him. For this, I am thankful. While it hurts to cut out the things that cause a divided heart, it in no way equals the pain and disappointment we endure when we realize we could have had more with God.

We all need to do a gut check. Just how far will we go?

- If God asked you to turn down the big promotion you have been working hard to get because the new job would cut into your time with him and your family, would you do it?
- If God asked you to give your last one hundred dollars to a family who was struggling, would you give it?
- If God asked you to sacrifice watching an entire season of your favorite sport to spend more time with him, would you do it?
- If God asked you to take your one free night a week and use it to invest in the lives of younger men at church, would you?
- If God wanted you to give up your place of leadership at your church and the esteem that goes with it to spend time strengthening your walk with him, would you resign your post?

It's easy to shout out, "Yes, I'll go all the way with God." It is a totally different thing when you see actual examples of what may be required of you when you make this commitment. Too many men jump headfirst into putting on manhood, only to return to their childish ways when they see what it actually requires.

There is a reason Jesus said, *But small is the gate and narrow the road that leads to life, and only a few find it* (Matthew 7:14). The Christian walk is hard. It isn't always candy canes and gumdrops. It takes commitment, sacrifice, and perseverance. It takes sticking to our guns and moving forward with God no matter how hard it is or how much he asks. But there is no better road to be on than the road to godly manhood. The question is, will you travel it?

Will you put on godly manhood, no matter what the cost? Like Joshua said many years ago, count the cost; don't dive in if you're not committed to making it a new way of life. If you think it will be too hard, then stay in your immaturity and squeak into heaven by the skin of your teeth. But if you are serious about following God, if you want to become all he can make you into, and if you will do whatever he asks, go wherever he leads, and sacrifice whatever he asks for, you will be able to put on manhood.

So the question I ask today is this: how far are you willing to go with God? Will you go all the way and serve him wholeheartedly, no matter the cost? If so, you have taken the first step to putting on manhood.

GROUP STUDY QUESTIONS

1. What are some things that have kept you from following God wholeheartedly?

2. What can you do to eliminate these barriers?

3. What are some of the cultural gods keeping you from whole-heartedly following God?

4. What are generational issues that keep you from following God without reservation?

5. This chapter listed some areas God may ask you to submit to him…what are some other things God may ask of you to get you to serve him with all your heart?

6. What can the group do to help you wholeheartedly serve God?

·3·

ROCKS, GRAVEL, SAND, AND WATER

As we look at the things in our lives which keep us from putting on manhood, one issue that keeps showing up is *having our priorities out of order*. We aren't looking at things through God's perspective of what is important or valuable. We spend our lives spinning our wheels as we pursue the things we want, the things we think we need, or the things we think will fulfill a longing deep inside of us. However, this takes our eyes off the important things and stunts our growth, spiritually, from childhood to manhood. So to put on manhood, we need to get our priorities straight.

Our culture has totally lost sight of what it means to have proper priorities. We place work and success too high on the list. We have put possessions and things in the wrong place. Play and entertainment are not in their proper position. These things have taken over the priorities in our life. A walk with God, family life, and investing in others have been bumped down the list.

One of my favorite stories is by Stephen Covey. It's about a time management expert who was speaking to a group of business students, and, to make a point, he used an illustration those students will never forget. As he stood in front of the group of high-powered over-achievers, he said,

"Okay, time for a quiz."

Then he pulled out a one-gallon, wide-mouthed mason jar and set it on a table in front of him. Then he produced about a dozen fist-sized rocks and carefully placed them, one at a time, into the jar. When the jar was filled to the top and no more rocks would fit inside, he asked, "Is the jar full?"

Everyone in the class said, "Yes."

Then he said, "Really?"

He reached under the table and pulled out a bucket of gravel. Then he dumped some gravel in and shook the jar, causing pieces of gravel to work themselves down into the space between the big rocks.

Then he smiled and asked the group once more, "Is the jar full?"

By this time the class was on to him.

"Probably not," one of them answered.

"Good!" he replied. And he reached under the table and brought out a bucket of sand. He started dumping the sand in and it went into all the spaces left between the rocks and the gravel. Once more he asked the question, "Is this jar full?"

"No!" the class shouted.

Once again he said, "Good!"

Then he grabbed a pitcher of water and began to pour it in until the jar was filled to the brim. Then he looked up at the class and asked, "What is the point of this illustration?"

One eager beaver raised his hand and said, "The point is, no matter how full your schedule is, if you try really hard, you can always fit some more things into it!"

"No," the speaker replied, "that's not the point. The truth this illustration teaches us is this: If you don't put the big rocks in first, you'll never get them in at all."

That's the point of this chapter. We are going to help you see what the "big rocks" need to be in your life. We need to identify what the things are in our life that we need to put in the jar first, because if they don't go in first, we will never get them into our daily lives.

So what are the big rocks?

PRIORITY NUMBER ONE: GOD

Our number one priority in life, the one thing that takes precedence over anything else, even family, needs to be God. He is the biggest rock, and he needs to go into the jar first to make sure he gets in at all. Unfortunately, many men make him the last thing they add to the jar, and they never seem to be able to squeeze him into their lives.

So many men constantly say they struggle to find time to read the Bible and pray. Life is too fast paced. Too much is going on. Prayer and Bible reading can be pushed aside for other more pressing things. They don't stop to realize what they are really saying is the cares of the world are more important to them than God. God isn't a big rock in their lives.

Spending time in the Word and spending time in prayer are the two main parts to becoming a godly man. So many men are trying to pursue becoming godly men without using these two parts, and they are getting nowhere.

Think about this. If you decide to take your boat out to the lake to go fishing, but you leave the motor and the oars on the shore, you are not going to be able to navigate the boat through the water, and you will float aimlessly on the lake. Men are not reading the Bible or praying, yet they wonder why they are struggling to stay afloat in their Christian lives.

We need to be men who commit ourselves to spending time with God, and we need to make this our number one priority. We need to set a time in our schedule that is untouchable. This is our time to develop our walk with God. During this time, we need to read God's Word and learn what he wants to change inside of us and to learn what his will is for our lives.

We need to spend time in the Bible so we can learn how to be better fathers and husbands. We need to read the Word to see how we can be better employees and better friends to those around us. The Bible needs to become our guidebook for life. So we need to schedule time into our day that is devoted to time spent in the Word. It needs to be untouchable time we refuse to miss.

We also need to block off time in our planners to spend alone with God in prayer. It's rightly been said that the number one sign of a godly man is calloused knees.

James 5:16 says *The prayer of a righteous person is powerful and effective.* There is power when God's men pray. Our prayers could change the world if only we took time to pray them. Satan knows it. This is why he will attempt anything to keep us from connecting with God in prayer. He knows how powerful it is because he knows how powerful God is and that God will back us up when we ask him for help.

Our number one priority in life, the one thing that takes precedence over anything else, needs to be God. He is the biggest rock, and he needs to go into the jar first to make sure he gets in at all.

Prayer is how we keep our spiritual lives alive. We have to keep our spiritual fire burning. The main fuel for this fire is prayer.

Prayer is a lot like a gas grill we use to cook our food when we barbecue. God is the propane tank that supplies the fuel, the passion, the fire. We are the grill that cooks the food, which does the work of ministry, witnessing, serving, and living our lives for God. Prayer is the gas line that connects the tank to the grill.

Without the gas line, the tank has no way to fuel the grill. The gas line connects the two parts together and produces a flame. When we pray, our prayers connect us to the heart of God. God gives us what we need to serve him and reach others with the gospel. If we don't make time in prayer a big rock in the jar, we lose a vital asset at our disposal to help us put on manhood.

You may say, "Jamie, I just don't see time in my life that I can use to read the Bible and pray. My day is full from the time I get up until the time I go to bed." This will sound blunt, but in reality, what you are saying is other things in your life are more important to you than the God who saved you from your sins and set you free. I don't say this to be hard or to make you feel guilty. I say it to add some perspective and show you why it is wrong to not make God your number one priority.

We all have things we can eliminate from our lives to spend time with God. I know in my life, I had to sacrifice time playing video games. I was a huge computer-golf fan. Because of my physical disabilities, I can no longer play golf for real, but on a computer I could not only play golf, but I could play on the finest, most exclusive courses in the world. However, as Mantour Ministries has grown, accompanied by the various ways I serve at our church, I had less and less free time in life. Instead of sacrificing the time I spend with God, I sacrifice the time I used to spend playing a game. My walk with God is eternal. The ministry I do helps others. A video game has no eternal value, so it was what had to go.

> **The number one sign of a godly man are calloused knees! There is power when God's men pray!**

These are the kinds of tough decisions you have to make to put away your childish things and put on manhood. You have to look at your life and identify the gravel and sand in your life, those things that eat up time but have no real importance. Maybe your Facebook time could be replaced with Bible reading time. Maybe the time you spend on the church softball team could become your prayer time. Maybe you really don't have any free time and nothing that can be replaced…if this is the case, you need to give up some sleep and get up earlier to spend time with God. God needs to become the biggest rock in your jar.

PRIORITY NUMBER TWO: OUR FAMILIES

The second big rock, or the next priority we need to focus on is our families.

You're probably thinking, "What, not my career?" No, your family needs to come before your career.

Your second most important responsibility as a man of God is to lead and guide your family. You are to be a godly role model for them to follow. Your wife should be able to rely on you for spiritual guidance, and your kids should see in you how to have a walk with God. That is why our relationship with God comes first. You need to have a relationship with God so you can effectively shoulder your second responsibility, your family.

> **Your second most important responsibility as a man of God is to lead and guide your family.**

So many men are missing out on being fathers and husbands because their priorities are out of whack. Men are pursuing power and money, and their families are living like widows and fatherless children. We are raising another generation of children who don't know how to develop a relationship with God, because they aren't seeing it modeled to them at home. Men miss out on their children's lives, thinking they will always have time to spend with their kids once they meet the next goal.

We assume we will always have time to spend with our families. However, talk to anyone who has experienced an unexpected tragedy in his life or lost someone close to him, and ask if time is a guaranteed commodity. I have heard my own father voice regrets of things he wish he had changed or ways he had treated my mom better while she was alive. He always thought he would have time in the future to do it, but then she died unexpectedly, and he was left living in regret about how he prioritized his life. He learned the hard way the importance of making your family a big rock in your jar. Fortunately, you don't have to learn this lesson the hard way. We can all choose to give our families their proper place in our lives, directly below God and on top of everything else.

PRIORITY NUMBER THREE: OUR JOBS

The next priority is your job. Like I said, we are not to neglect our jobs. God wants us all to be faithful workers. However, he also wants us to keep our job in perspective. It is a part of our lives, not all of it.

A job is a way to provide the things your family needs. Too many men pursue the buck, the promotion, the success, at the expense of their family. In the end, they have lots of prestige in the business world, but are failures in their personal lives. Our jobs are not meant to be the place we have all our needs met. Unfortunately many men try to get their self-worth and significance through their work. Their job becomes who they are. However, this can't be.

> **Your job isn't where you get your identity. It isn't where you get your self-esteem. It's where you get your currency to provide for your family.**

Your job isn't where you get your identity. It isn't where you get your self-worth. You get that first and foremost from God, then your wife and kids. A job is where you get your currency to provide. It is where you trade your skill for the paper needed to provide the needs of your family and to help grow God's kingdom through your tithe and your influence on co-workers. To place it as anything more important in your life is wrong.

That's not to say you don't give your full effort at your job or you're a poor steward over your career. God wants all of us to be responsible workers. He wants us to do all we can to help our employers and companies. When we are responsible with our jobs, we are good examples for God. We will stand out among the crowd. People will see we are different and God will receive praise because of our actions. So we need to be good workers and faithful employees who keep our jobs in focus. We do good work at work, but we also know when it is quitting time and we then re-focus on God and our family.

These are the three big rocks that need to take the rightful spot in your life's jar. God needs to be first, then your family, then your career. There is still one more big rock we need to discuss.

PRIORITY NUMBER FOUR: MENTORSHIP/DISCIPLESHIP

The fourth big rock, the fourth thing that has to take priority in our lives, is mentorship/discipleship. **Every man needs to have someone mentoring him, and every man needs to be mentoring someone else.** After Jesus rose from the dead, he gave his disciples a command before he returned to his rightful place in heaven. Matthew 28:18–20 says:

> *Then Jesus came to them and said, "All authority in heaven and on earth has been given to me. Therefore go and make disciples of all nations, baptizing them in the name of the Father and of the Son and of the Holy Spirit, and teaching them to obey everything I have commanded you."*

This passage has been called the Great Commission, but for too long God's men have been treating it like it's the Great Option. But the word Jesus used is "Go." "Go" is an action verb. It means do it. Jesus didn't say, "Try and squeeze some time in to reach the lost or to disciple younger believers." He said, "Do it!"

Witnessing, mentoring, and discipleship need to become a big rock in our lives. We're going to talk more about this later in the book, but we need to mention here it is not something we squeeze into our lives; it needs to take precedence. Very few men of God have done great things for him without having first been influenced and trained by other men. Our job is to seek the wisdom and guidance of older men who have experienced the hard knocks in life and learn from them how to avoid these traps. Then, in turn, we do the same for someone else.

We need to give priority to these four big rocks if we are going to put on manhood. After these four things have taken precedence in your life, then the other things, the trivial things, the gravel, sand, and water, can fill up the rest. They are the things that get pushed aside when our schedule gets full or we run out of time. Things like entertainment, play, sports, fantasy football, social networking, hunting, and other less important things will fit around the important things.

This is what it takes to put away childish things and to put on manhood. The question is, how far are you willing to go for God? Will you get your priorities straight? Will you fill your jar with the big rocks first? Only you can answer these questions. But you need to decide today!

GROUP STUDY QUESTIONS

1. What are the big rocks in your life right now? What changes do you need to make to take these rocks out of your life and put the proper big rocks in the jar?

2. Is spending time with God a big rock in your life? If not, what steps can you take to make this a priority?

3. What can you sacrifice to make time spent with God a priority? How can we as a group help you keep this commitment?

4. This chapter made the statement, "Your wife should be able to rely on you for spiritual guidance, and your kids should see in you how to have a walk with God." What would your wife and kids say if they were asked this question?

5. Do you use your career to meet needs inside of you?

6. Is mentorship/discipleship a big rock in your life?

7. Who is discipling you, and who are you discipling?

8. What can we as a group do to help you get your priorities straight and keep them straight?

·4·

WHO ARE YOU?

Recently, I was involved in a conversation with some friends, and one of the guys was sharing his testimony. During the course of the conversation, he made a statement that really hit home.

He said "Show me who you spend your time with and I will show you who you are."

The point he was making was that who we spend time with is who we become like, and where we spend our time influences who we are.

This is so true. Hang with immoral people and soon you will be doing immoral things. If you spend your time with dishonest people, you will begin practicing deceit. Spend all your time in front of a TV or movie screen watching less-than-holy Hollywood trash, and you will soon have a life filled with trash.

The Bible says the same idea in 1 Corinthians 15:33 when Paul says, *Do not be misled: "Bad company corrupts good character."* The obvious counterpoint to this is good company will encourage good character. This brings us to the next area we need to work on when putting on godly manhood.

To grow in our walk with God, we need to be devoted to the things of God. You may wonder what the difference is between being devoted to the things of God, and following God wholeheartedly, as we discussed in Chapter Two. I'm glad you asked, because there is a huge difference.

In Chapter Two, we discussed the need to have a personal relationship with God. We saw that this involves our personal walk with God, our prayer life, our Bible reading, and our development of an intimate, one-on-one relationship with God. Being devoted to God is different. In order to see the difference, let's look at the book of Acts.

I love the book of Acts. It tells us about the beginning of the church, and it is filled with stories of men and women of God who were used mightily to spread the gospel to others. The amazing accounts of how the Holy Spirit flowed through these men and women as they preached the gospel to all the nations of the world are some of the most powerful and exciting passages in the Bible. However, before these people set the world on fire, they devoted themselves to God.

Acts 2:42 says *They devoted themselves to the apostles' teaching and to fellowship, to the breaking of bread and to prayer.* The first church, the early believers, devoted themselves to a corporate time together worshipping God and learning his Word together. They saw the importance of being part of a spiritual body of believers who learned, shared, and grew together. They focused specific time to get together and study the Word, to fellowship, and for corporate prayer. Men, we need to do the same.

A man of God is committed to his local church. We all need to be part of a Bible-believing church. Unfortunately, churches are not the most prominent place to find men. Our churches are being run mostly by women. In most churches, women teach Sunday school. Women have huge turnout for their women's ministries. Meanwhile, men's ministries are struggling to get any men to turn out. Churches are desperate for male leaders, but men aren't making church involvement a part of their lives.

Now, I want to make one thing clear. I am not a male chauvinist pig. I have no problem with women ministering or being involved in a church. I believe women should be able to do whatever they want to do. However, *want* is the key word. They should desire to do it. They shouldn't be forced to do it because men aren't willing to be responsible and dependable, to step up and serve in the church. We need to address this area in our lives. It is time men start being devoted to God through their local church.

We need to be willing to give of ourselves for the benefit of the church. We must be open and honest with others, sharing not only our strengths but also our weaknesses. We can't go to church with our walls up. We must go in and be vulnerable, sharing our lives with others so we can help them in their own walk with God. We also have to be teachable so other believers can influence our lives.

As you can see, I am talking about more than just filling a seat in church. God has more than enough suits sitting in pews. He is looking for men who go from sitting in the pew, taking from others, to men who are willing to give to other believers in the church and help them.

We show our devotion to God when we come alongside the younger men in our church. Guys, our churches are full of young men who are growing up without a man in their lives. Whether it's through divorce, abandonment, absentee dads, or dads being workaholics, there is a generation of young men out there starving for male attention

> **God is looking for men who go from sitting in a pew, taking from others, to men who are willing to give to other believers in the church and help them.**

and for someone to show them what it means to be a godly man and how to live in God's kingdom. Part of being devoted to God is helping these younger men by being a positive influence in their lives.

You see, putting on manhood isn't just about us. It involves how we interact with other people. So a man of God is devoted to the things of God, and is actively involved in a body of believers.

Why do we need to do this? Because we need to be learning from each other. We need the support and encouragement. We need to learn to invest in others and have others invest in us. No man can be an island in his walk with God. He needs other people around him.

You may be thinking, "Jamie, I get what you're saying, but I don't feel like I am equipped to preach or teach at my church. Is this the only way to show my devotion?"

I am so glad you asked that question. Being active in a local church doesn't mean you have to be a preacher or a teacher. There are so many important and necessary areas in which you could help a church. Honestly, any talent or ability you have could be used as a gift of service to your church. What do I mean?

For instance, if you are mechanically inclined or enjoy working on cars, you could volunteer to keep the church vans running. If you are artistic, you could paint pictures and murals in the children's area of the church. Do you enjoy gardening? Volunteer to plant flowers, pull weeds, mow the lawn, and other outdoor projects at the church property. Are you handy? Then build sets for your pastor's next sermon series that add visual illustrations to his sermon. Do you like kids? Offer to provide babysitting for the women's group so moms can attend and not have to hire a babysitter. Are you a plumber? Church toilets and pipes clog too; fix them. No matter what your gift, talent, interest, or hobby, there is a way you can use it to help your local body of believers. You can influence others and show your devotion to God without ever standing behind a podium.

I think too often people take the privilege of going to church and being a part of a body of believers for granted. I for one am a man who greatly appreciates the opportunity to be part of a local church. Why?

I went through a period of time when it was literally impossible for me to go to church. My mom had extreme allergies to perfumes and other scents. Her lungs would close and she would have to be rushed to the doctor so she could breathe. Because of this, it was out of the question for her to go to church. And because of the abusive way my father treated her, it was not safe to leave her alone with him, and his days off were always during times when there were church services. So in order to protect her, I was unable to attend church. Only through personal Bible study and radio ministries was I able to stay spiritually fed. However, being part of a body of believers was not possible, and I missed it!

After my mom went to spend eternity with Jesus, I began to attend a local church again. I am so thankful for the privilege to attend a church, to be fed the Word through teaching, to take Communion, but, most of all, to have relationships with other believers who are just as devoted to their walk with God as I am to mine. It is a privilege and an honor to spend time with these people as we devote ourselves to God together.

Can you say the same thing? Are you devoted to the things of God? Is gathering together with other believers to learn more about God and his kingdom important to you? Are you giving of yourself, your time, and your abilities to your church? Not everyone will be a teacher or a preacher in a church body, but everyone has something to offer. We all have unique abilities and gifts that can be used to benefit each other. Are you using your unique gifts to help others?

This is a vital part of a Christian's walk. We live in childish ways when we neglect a body of believers, but we are putting on manhood when we devote ourselves to God. Which will you choose?

GROUP STUDY QUESTIONS

1. The chapter discussed the quote "Show me who you spend your time with, and I will show you who you are." How does this quote apply to your life before you got saved?

2. How does this quote apply to your life now?

3. What is the difference between following God wholeheartedly and being devoted to God?

4. How devoted to God are you?

5. What are some ways you can become more active in your church?

6. What are some unique gifts and abilities you have, and how could they benefit the church you attend?

7. What can we as a group do to help you grow in your devotion to God?

·5·

THE BIG A

I love to travel. I enjoy being on the open road, radio blasting, as I sing at the top of my lungs—okay, I'm the only one who enjoys the last part. I especially enjoy trips where the destinations are men's events and ministry.

Recently, I had the privilege of teaching a workshop at a large men's convention in Pennsylvania. It was a great experience and an amazing conference. The main speakers were excellent, and we got to meet a lot of great men and introduce them to Mantour Ministries. It was especially rewarding because it was close to home, and I got to be with a few of my church friends at the same time.

I especially loved the theme the conference leaders chose for this convention. It was called *The Band of Brothers*. This theme brings us to the next area in which we need to put away childish things and put on manhood.

Let's face it, we all need each other. No man can walk alone through his spiritual journey. Only someone living in childish ways would even try it. It's like the little kid who refuses help and direction but loudly screams "I can do it myself!" This is immature and childish.

A real man focused on putting on manhood understands he needs other men who stand alongside him as they travel together toward becoming godly men. He has a band of brothers to whom he is accountable and who he, in turn, holds accountable.

Guys, we need to have other men in our lives. No man is an island! We can't Lone Ranger our way through life. Heck, the Lone Ranger didn't even fly solo; he had Tonto!

Our band of brothers supply support to us. They provide a way for us to have accountability. We all need to be accountable to each other. Our band of brothers are men we can trust to look us in the eye and say, "Your priorities are out of whack."

> **No man is an island. Even the Lone Ranger didn't fly solo; he had Tonto!**

They can say to us, "Bro, you need to make a change here."

They can smack us upside the head and say, "What were you thinking?!"

They are men we are completely open with who can ask us anything they want.

Did that last point freak you out a bit? I know it did when I re-read it. There is a part of every one of us that gets uncomfortable letting men into every area of our life. Let's face it, we all have areas we wish we could keep to ourselves, areas we don't want anyone to know about. We fear what their reaction will be or how they will judge us. So we hide these areas inside of us, throw a lock on them, and never let anyone see them. But what good does this do?

Does it help us overcome? Does it bring us freedom? Do we gain support and strength to deal with these issues? No. All it does is keep them safe, protected, and untouched. Like food inside of Tupperware, these areas stay fresh and active inside of us. But this is a bad thing! We never overcome, change, or grow.

God's will for all of his children is to throw off daily the sins that so easily entangle us and to be formed into the image of his Son, Jesus. One great tool we have at our disposal to help us accomplish this goal is to have a band of brothers who come alongside and help us.

I am so grateful for the band of brothers God has blessed me with. I don't know what I'd do without them! They are always there for me when I need them.

A few years ago, a good friend of mine went through a very difficult time, and unfortunately, this friend became very bitter. Over time, the anger and bitterness became like a poison, contaminating everyone who came in contact with this person.

This friend's behavior began to affect me. I started to struggle to follow God down certain paths he was leading me. I began looking at certain people through my bitter friend's eyes, not God's eyes. I was sinking fast.

One of the guys in my band of brothers and his wife kindly confronted me and showed me that I was in trouble. He helped me see how this friend's bitterness was affecting me, and he lovingly pointed me away from this mindset and back to what God had called me to do.

This is what it's all about, men helping men. Such men help us grow in our walk with God. They point out areas of sin inside of us, help us see them, and encourage us to grow and overcome!

Peter had such a friend. The Bible tells us Peter was a man who loved to eat ham! Peter was a bacon guy just like me! However, a good Jew didn't dare eat bacon, so when Peter was around Jews, he acted like he hated pork, but when he was around Gentiles, it was BLTs and pork rinds nonstop!

Paul loved Peter enough to pull him aside and show him this was sin. Galatians 2:11–14 says:

> *Later, when Peter came to Antioch, I had a face-to-face confrontation with him because he was clearly out of line. Here's the situation. Earlier, before certain persons had come from James, Peter regularly ate with the non-Jews. But when that conservative group came from Jerusalem, he cautiously pulled back and put as much distance as he could manage between himself and his non-Jewish friends. That's how fearful he was*

of the conservative Jewish clique that's been pushing the old system of circumcision. Unfortunately, the rest of the Jews in the Antioch church joined in that hypocrisy so that even Barnabas was swept along in the charade.

But when I saw that they were not maintaining a steady, straight course according to the Message, I spoke up to Peter in front of them all: "If you, a Jew, live like a non-Jew when you're not being observed by the watchdogs from Jerusalem, what right do you have to require non-Jews to conform to Jewish customs just to make a favorable impression on your old Jerusalem cronies?" (The Message).

We need such men in our lives, men who will point out areas of sin and show us what we need to change. We also need them so we have someone to reach out to in times of trouble. When the going gets tough, we need men in our lives we can cry out to and say, "I am in a battle; I need help! Will you fight with me?"

Jesus did this while on earth. On the night he knew he would be betrayed, he took his three closest friends aside and asked them to support him.

Then Jesus went with his disciples to a place called Gethsemane, and he said to them, "Sit here while I go over there and pray." He took Peter and the two sons of Zebedee along with him, and he began to be sorrowful and troubled. Then he said to them, "My soul is overwhelmed with sorrow to the point of death. Stay here and keep watch with me." (Matthew 26:36–38)

Jesus knew what he would face that night, and he wanted his closest friends to help him get through it.

Paul also looked for men to come alongside him during his times of trial. Throughout the book of Acts, we see Paul constantly surrounding himself with men who helped him through the hard times he faced. When facing his darkest hour, awaiting his death at the hands of an insane dictator, Nero, he reached out to his friends to support him. 2 Timothy 4:9–11 says, *Do your best to come to me quickly…Only Luke is with me. Get Mark and bring him with you, because he is helpful to me in my ministry.* Facing a time of trial, Paul wanted to gather his men around him for help and support.

I really don't know what I would do without my band of brothers. I remember one time when I was facing a really tough situation, and I honestly didn't know which way to go. I immediately dropped an e-mail to my guys, asked for support and prayer. Within a minute, my phone rang. It was one of my guys calling to help me. Over the next few days, these men held me up in prayer, and I could feel their prayers making a difference.

Just recently, I had a minor physical crisis in my life. For those of you who have never met me in person, I have a physical handicap that causes me to walk with a bad limp and live in constant pain. Another side effect is that the way I walk causes me to develop *severe* calluses on my foot. This physical issue is a genetic disease. My dad has it, his dad had it, and without God's intervention, my future kids will have it.

However, I have a promise from God, a spiritual word of knowledge that someday I will be healed, and that this disease will not go on to another generation. As confirmation that this word is true, God healed one of my feet, which, at the time, was in worse shape than the one I still struggle with daily. So I have a promise from God, and one healed foot to confirm it.

Recently though, I had an issue with my bad foot where the callus that built up tore off from my foot, leaving a gaping, painful wound. Years ago, my dad had an issue with his bad foot. He got ulcers growing on it that got infected, and it was *years* of treatment and pain until they recovered. The callus that tore off my foot was in the *exact* same spot on the foot that he had developed his ulcer. As soon as I saw my wound, I was consumed with fear. It crippled me. Fear stopped me dead in my tracks.

I was attacked with thoughts from the enemy, "Your foot is never going to get better. You're going to end up in a wheelchair. You may as well give up waiting on God and believing him. He won't come through!"

Now, I am usually pretty good at discerning the enemy's attacks...I don't say that proudly; it is spiritual discernment working inside of me. However, this time, I was too terrified to discern it. I was in big trouble, I was getting the tar beat out of me by the enemy, and I was slipping fast.

Throughout my life, I have handled my physical issues in a very childish way. I screamed like a child, "I can handle this myself! I don't want help, and I don't want others knowing about my disease!" But this time I was crippled with terror, so I decided to practice what I preach and turn to my band of brothers.

I had a heartfelt talk with one of them. I told him everything: my insecurities, my fears, the terror, everything. He comforted me, prayed with me, but most importantly, he helped regain my focus and my faith in God to do what he promised in his timing. He helped me out by giving me faith when I had none of my own. He was there for me and he got me through. Two weeks later, the wound was healed and I was fine.

Guys, this is why we need a band of brothers. Like a wounded soldier needs his band of brothers to hoist him on their shoulders and carry him to safety, we need men to carry us spiritually when we are too weak or wounded to make it through the battle on our own. I was drowning in my spiritual battle, and he grabbed me by the shoulders and helped me to a place of safety.

Our band of brothers is also there to give us wisdom and advice as we go through our daily lives. We need men around us to teach us. Older saints can help the younger saints. There is no trial or temptation that is new under the sun, and it's time for God's men to be open and vulnerable and admit to our struggles and weaknesses so we can support each other.

We can learn from others how to gain victories or avoid defeats. A band of brothers can help each other by saying, "I struggled with this area, and I learned this going through it. Now here is how you avoid making the same mistake."

Remember earlier when I told the story of the friend and his wife who helped me deal with the effects another friend's hatred and anger was having on me? Why were they able to pick up on it and recognize I needed help? Because they had faced a similar situation in their past, and because of this they could see where I was heading. Instead of letting me learn the hard way, they used their own experience to help me avoid what they endured. My friends, that is what God calls all of us to do!

I have a young friend who is starting the road to ministry. God has allowed me to help steer him along the path toward discovering the call on his life. I have been able to help him avoid some of the mistakes I made. I have been able to give him guidance as to what path to take or what decisions to make based on my own personal experiences. I don't say this to make myself look good. I say it to show how God can use us.

Why should this young man have to strive and struggle when I have gone through the same thing?

I've had older guys do the same for me. A few weeks ago, I had an opportunity to try a type of outreach that I hadn't done before. This was a *huge* opportunity for me. The man who invited me, a good friend of mine, sat in on my outreach. Halfway through, he came up front and began co-teaching with me. Honestly, I was shocked and instantly I thought, "Wow, I blew it! He didn't like how I handled this situation, and he took it over."

A band of brothers can help each other by saying, "I struggled with this area, and I learned this going through it. Now here is how you avoid making the same mistake.

I was crushed. I felt like I blew a big opportunity. I felt like a failure. I didn't get a chance to talk to this guy after the meeting as we both were mobbed with men asking us questions, but late that night, he called me on the phone. He explained to me what had happened.

He always intended to interrupt and take part in the class because he wanted to help me learn. Then, he went on to show how he had orchestrated everything about the outreach, the crowd size, the topic, everything, so that I would succeed and also learn from him for future events. I went from feeling like a failure to feeling loved and protected by a father-like figure.

I will never, ever forget how this man invested in me and made sure I learned in a safe environment, while giving me a chance to grow and succeed. He poured into me what he had learned over the years, just like I am pouring into this younger guy as he begins down the path of ministry. *That* is what it is all about, men helping men. Mentoring. Going on a Mantour, where you show other men what you learned on your journey into manhood. That is the heart of Mantour Ministries: Men traveling together on the road to godly manhood!

Every man needs a man older than him mentoring him, and every man needs to be mentoring other younger guys. We need to work together and help each other on this journey along the Christian life.

What about you? Do you have men in your life who are investing in you, showing you ways to avoid the same mistakes and failures they encountered?

Are there younger guys in your life you can do the same for as they go through their walk with God?

Do you have men you can contact for help when going through tough times?

Are there men in your life who will love you enough to stare you straight in the eyes and say, "Bro, you're in trouble. Stop what you are doing"?

We all need men in our life like this. If you don't have such men in your life, start asking God to send them into your life.

Start attending a Bible-believing church. You will connect with other believers who can disciple you and help you along your spiritual journey. You will meet younger guys you can invest in as they grow in God.

If you are not already attending a men's group, I recommend you connect with one at your church. If your church doesn't have a men's ministry, contact me and I'll help you get one started or connect you to other groups who can help.

Accountability with a band of brothers is a key part of putting on manhood. The question I have for you today is this: will you continue in your childish ways, insisting you can handle it yourself, or will you put on manhood and develop a band of brothers and enter into accountability relationships? In my opinion, there is only one choice, but you need to be the one to choose. I urge you to choose today!

GROUP STUDY QUESTIONS

1. "No man is an island." What does this statement mean to you?

2. Does the thought of having men in your life who can ask you anything or hold you accountable freak you out? Why?

3. Why is it important for you to have an older man invest in you?

4. Who is someone older who has invested in your life?

5. How has his investment benefited your life?

6. Do you invest yourself in the life of a younger man?

7. Who is a younger guy you could invest in?

·6·

YANKING YOUR ROOTS

Do you like to garden? Many men love to garden, whether it's to add curb appeal gardening around their home, or old-school, grow-your-own-veggies gardening. I am not one of these men! To be honest with you, gardening is not a hobby of mine. I don't have the patience it takes to be a good gardener. Why do I say that?

One reason is because I live at the base of a mountain, and any produce I would try to grow would turn into a hot date night for a huge eight-point buck and his lady. Deer, rabbits, squirrels, and other woodland animals would visit our buffet and eat it all, leaving me nothing for my hard work. However, a bigger reason is because when you plant a produce garden, it takes *forever* for the fruit to grow. I just don't have the patience to wait.

Curb appeal gardening doesn't appeal to me either for one reason… weeds! It seems like for every flower you grow, ten weeds grow around it. I have some gardens in my yard that have mulch covering them and some with decorative rocks covering them, and they always end up being a great source of frustration to me because of weeds.

I've tried everything to get rid of them. I tried using a weed whacker, but all this does is trim them down. It doesn't get rid of the weeds; it just makes them look good.

I tried using a natural mixture made of soap, vinegar, salt, and water. The person who gave me the recipe said it was *guaranteed* to kill my weeds. This concoction killed the weeds above the ground, shriveling up the weed and turning it brown. But since it didn't kill the root of the weed, it will eventually grow back.

I have found the only way to get rid of a weed is to bend down, grab it, and yank it out of the ground, roots and all. Once the root of the weed is gone, it's unable to grow. It is dead, it is gone, and it won't be an issue anymore. But it takes a lot of hard work and patience to pull a zillion weeds, so I am ashamed to say I often tolerate the weeds and just trim them, keeping them looking good and presentable. However, the weed is still there, and if I ever go away, or miss a week of weed whacking, it will grow and corrupt the garden again, becoming an eyesore.

> It is time God's men stop living in this childish behavior and start putting on manhood! We do this by once and for all facing the unforgiveness and pain in our lives and allowing the Holy Spirit to heal us.

I wonder how many of us do the same in our spiritual lives. Do you know the number one sin men struggle with? I am sure your mind went directly to the big Ps: pornography and pride. However, this isn't the answer. The number one issue is rage.

Does this answer surprise you? It did me, but when you stop and really think about it, it is true. How often does the news media report stories of men murdering wives or girlfriends? Murder is the extreme end of the rage. More common is physical abuse, verbal abuse, screaming fits, tantrums, and many other manifestations that destroy our relationships.

Men are having fits of anger and rage around the world, resulting in abuse, scars, broken marriages, broken families, and broken relationships. Calls for tougher gun laws are being shouted out across the country.

We need to stop trimming the rage weed with a weed whacker, or squirting the rage with a weed killer. All this does is make the rage look better or hide it. If we are to be men of God who are daily putting on manhood, we need to get to the root of our rage, and yank it out once and for all. Only then can we live free of our anger and rage, and become calm, compassionate, loving men of God.

So what is the root of rage? Rage is just out-of-control hatred and anger. It is the result of anger issues we allowed to develop in our lives. So to yank the weed of rage, we need to identify the leaves of anger and hate. But to deal with these issues, we need to go even lower on the weed and see what is going on underground. We need to discover the root and yank it out at the base.

The root of almost all anger, hate, and rage is unforgiveness. Someone in your life did something to you and it hurt you and caused you pain. Instead of facing the pain, dealing with it, and forgiving the person who hurt you, many of us deny the pain, deny the action hurt us, and we ignore the pain. We bury the pain inside our hearts. However, because the weed was not killed, it takes root in our heart and slowly it grows, blossoming into anger, hatred, and rage. Instead of dealing with the pain, we become a hateful, cruel person who explodes at the slightest injury. Afterward, we are left devastated and alone, wondering why we just did what we did as we see the ones we love hurting and suffering around us.

Guys, it is time God's men stop living in this childish behavior and start putting on manhood! We do this by once and for all facing the unforgiveness and pain in our lives and allowing the Holy Spirit to heal us.

Maybe you are thinking, "Jamie, I can't do this. It hurts too much and I just don't have it in me to do it."

My answer to you is you are absolutely right! It does hurt to face the buried memories and forgive, and you don't have it in you to do it. However, you do have the Holy Spirit on your side, and he has the strength to do this work inside of you. How do I know? Because he did it in my life.

When people first meet me, they describe me as funny, kind, gentle, and caring. I am the guy who plays with the church kids, hugs the hurting, and shows mercy to others when they hurt me. Often, (and sometimes to my annoyance…ha-ha!), women see me as safe and a big brother in their lives. I don't say this to brag, because I know I am only this way through the power of the Holy Spirit. You see, I know what I used to be.

I used to be a boiling pot! I used to be the world's moodiest man. You never knew what you would get with me. One minute I was the life of the party, the next I was withdrawn, silent, and depressed. Anger ruled my life, and it didn't take much to make my hot temper explode. I was a powder keg of anger, rage, and hate. The problem was, I didn't know why. After an explosion when I would hurt those around me, I was just as confused as to why I exploded as those I exploded on.

Even as a young adult serving God and trying to be an effective minister, I would have fits of anger and rage. Instead of digging deep into my heart and finding the root of the action, I would weed whack the sin and keep it looking neat and presentable.

It looked good, and people would admire the good things surrounding the weeds in my heart, but the weeds never went away. They were still there, and they continued to grow and expose themselves from time to time. I was stuck in a mad cycle of loving and serving God, followed by outbursts of anger and rage, and then repentance and promises it would never happen again. But it just kept happening.

Finally, the mad cycle came to a head in my life. I'll never forget that night. I woke up in the middle of the night to a bloodcurdling scream. My mom had a nightmare that scared her so badly she jumped out of bed to run away. As she jumped up, she tripped and fell, injuring her shoulder. Scared, half-asleep, and in pain, she screamed for help. My sister and I jumped out of bed, ran to her side, and helped her.

At this point, my dad put in his two cents. He was angry at my mom for waking him. He showed no concern for her or her health. Instead, he verbally and emotionally abused a woman in pain.

His behavior infuriated me. I was so angry, I could have hit him! Instead, I turned and punched the hallway door, putting my fist through it. I was left with a broken door, a hurt hand, and a shattered heart.

I was devastated by my actions. I was angry at my father for being abusive, yet here I was acting just like him!

I instantly felt like God could never use me again since I was capable of this behavior. I cried for hours. I felt hopeless and ashamed. I felt the weeds of rage and hatred choking me to death. I knew the time had come to get to the root and deal with the issue once and for all.

I cried out to God for help. I begged the Holy Spirit to help me break free of hate, anger, and rage in my life. He answered me that he was waiting for me to ask, and he would love to do this work inside of me. However, I had to allow him to expose the hidden pain in my heart. I was so desperate to be different that I did what I had avoided doing for over twenty years. Finally, I faced the pain of abuse inside my heart, faced the anger, hate, and unforgiveness I had for my dad for causing me the pain, and chose once and for all to forgive him.

Now, I'm not going to lie to you and tell you it was a breeze. It *hurt*! The Holy Spirit reminded me of instances in my life I had blocked out in my mind and buried—painful times I never wanted to admit happened, or worse yet, face. I had to remember the words, the fists, the pain, the excruciating sense of rejection, and the mind control and brainwashing I had experienced. It was hard, I cried a lot of tears, and I hurt. But you know what? I also was set free and became a different man!

The Holy Spirit made me face the pain, and he helped me forgive my dad. He made me stop looking at my dad through the childish eyes of pain and see him through the eyes of a man. I saw how my father's actions were a result of the pain he experienced in his own life. Just like my actions and rage were the result of unforgiveness and unresolved issues, so were his. He experienced nightmares I couldn't imagine, and his actions toward me were actually his reaction to his own heart weeds.

When I began to allow the Holy Spirit to show this to me, I was able to let go of the pain. Why? Because I began to see if I didn't forgive him, I would continue through life chained to this sin, and I would follow his example and pass it on to another generation. If I wanted God to forgive me for my actions and show me compassion and mercy, then I needed to show my dad the same compassion and mercy. I had to become a forgiving man in order to put on godly manhood. The same is true for everyone.

You may be thinking, "I understand the importance of forgiveness, but I just don't feel like I can forgive this person. What can I do?"

Let me be the first to tell you this: there is hope. It doesn't matter if you feel you can't forgive someone. You can't wait for this feeling to come. Forgiveness is not an emotion. It is a mental decision you need to make. You must consciously decide, "I am going to forgive that person." It has to be a decision you make of your own free will.

When God first started dealing with me about the need to forgive others, he showed me I had to do it even if I didn't feel like it. I had to decide daily to forgive my dad.

It was hard. I didn't want to forgive. Then my mom told me a few ways she had learned to help change her heart to forgive. I used them and they helped. I'll share them with you.

The first thing she told me was to begin to ask God to bless the person you need to forgive.

Jesus commanded us to bless those who despitefully use us (Matthew 5:44). We need to follow this pattern. Ask God to bless the person, provide for his or her needs, and to help the person become all he wants them to be. It is hard to feel hatred and unforgiveness while praying for the person's good.

The second thing she taught me was to do something nice for the person, because Jesus taught us to do good to those who hate us (Luke 6:27).

Remember the last chapter when I told you about a foot injury my dad had developed? This injury required a clean bandage and cleansing every morning. It was on a spot of his foot he couldn't reach to apply the bandage, so God required me to get up each day and dress his wound, all the while still receiving his mean and abusive behavior. I did it for God and endured the treatment because I wanted to be free from any unforgiveness in my heart.

We need to try and find a way to do good for the person we have unforgiveness toward, even if it is as simple as buying the person a cup of coffee or helping do some home repair project. You will be able to do it. How do I know? Because Jesus did it.

If ever there was a man who had the right to harbor unforgiveness, it was Jesus. He was beaten, almost to death. He was mocked. He was spit upon. He was ridiculed, despised, and abused. He was hung on a cross even though he was totally innocent and sinless. He had every reason in the world to hate, be angry, and seek vengeance. He had every right in the world to destroy everyone around the cross for what they did to him, and he had the power and ability to do it. But he didn't; instead, he asked his Father to forgive them! He did good to his enemies. We need to do the same.

The third thing she taught me was you need to forgive the person; however, you can't condone his or her evil behavior.

Forgiveness doesn't mean you allow the person to keep sinning against you. I have, through the power of the Holy Spirit, forgiven my dad, but I do not allow him to abuse me. My forgiveness is not a license for him to be abusive. When he acts abusively, I lovingly confront him and let him know it is unacceptable and it *will not* continue. However, I don't allow hatred, anger, or unforgiveness to take root inside of me, either.

For instance, I remember the last time my dad had an extreme outburst. He meant to scare and intimidate my sister and me in order to get his own way. I didn't flip out on him or allow anger, rage, or unforgiveness to consume me. Instead, through the power of the Holy Spirit, I told him this behavior was unacceptable, and he had to stop and get control of himself. Then I went on with the rest of the day.

True forgiveness allows you to take a stand against the evil behavior while not allowing anger, bitterness, and hate to consume you. Forgiveness is as much for your own mental and spiritual condition as it is for the other person.

> **True forgiveness allows you to take a stand against the evil behavior while not allowing anger, bitterness, and hate to consume you.**

Lastly, seek out a Spirit-filled counselor who is qualified to help you recognize and deal with the root of your anger. God has given us these people who are trained and equipped to help us when we don't even know where to begin.

We need to be men of forgiveness. Forgiving kills sins of bitterness, hate, and anger and stops them from polluting our heart. It yanks the weed out of your heart instead of just keeping it well groomed, manicured, or hidden. We must all decide today we will put away our childish ways of holding onto anger, hate, rage, and unforgiveness. Instead, we choose to put on manhood and forgive.

GROUP STUDY QUESTIONS

1. Do you ever struggle with uncontrollable anger or rage?

2. What sets you off?

3. Have you been weed whacking your weeds of rage to make them look good instead of getting to the root?

4. What is keeping you from getting to the root?

5. Who are you holding unforgiveness toward?

6. This chapter suggests praying for the person you are unforgiving toward, doing something good for him or her, and forgiving without condoning the behavior. Which of these is hardest for you to do?

7. What can we as a group do to help you deal with your root of unforgiveness?

·7·

WALKING
UNDER THE INFLUENCE

For about four years, I taught Berean School of the Bible classes every week. One of the classes I taught was on the book of Acts. As I prepared the lessons each week, I couldn't help but notice the importance the early church placed on the power of the Holy Spirit. As I read the amazing stories, I started thinking how sad it is that we seem to have lost focus of the great power we have when we are filled with the Holy Spirit. In order to put on manhood, we need to rediscover the power of the Holy Spirit and how it can affect our lives.

Recently, I was going through an extremely busy day. I was swamped with work and was getting ready to leave for a short trip. As I rushed around, I felt God tell me I needed to contact a friend and check on how he was doing. I ignored this prompting and continued on with my busy day. As the day went on, the prompting from the Holy Spirit just got stronger, and after hours of ignoring that voice, it became so strong that I finally sat down at my computer and sent an e-mail to my friend. I told him I was thinking about him and was wondering how he was doing.

A few minutes later, I got a response saying my friend was really struggling. He was experiencing some physical and personal problems, and really needed some support. God knew this and used me to help him. Unfortunately, he had to go through the entire day without help because I ignored the Holy Spirit's initial prompting.

The Holy Spirit used this experience to teach me about the necessity of living a Spirit-led life and always obeying his voice. I learned it's better to err on the side of obedience than worry about whether or not I am hearing the voice of the Holy Spirit and disobey him. Since this experience, my prayer has become, "I want to live a Spirit-led life." In this chapter, I want to encourage each of you to make this your prayer as well.

Perhaps the best place to begin this discussion is by answering the question, "Who Is the Holy Spirit?"

Simply put, the Holy Spirit is the third member of the Godhead or Trinity. The Trinity consists of God the Father, Jesus the Son, and the Holy Spirit. As such, he has all the attributes of the Deity in that he is eternal, unchanging, all-powerful, present everywhere, and has all knowledge. As we study the Bible, we can see he played an active role throughout.

We are first introduced to the Holy Spirit at creation. Genesis 1:2 says, *And the earth was without form, and void; and darkness was upon the face of the deep. And the Spirit of God moved upon the face of the waters* (KJV).

Throughout the Old Testament, we see the Holy Spirit come upon various leaders, judges, and warriors, enabling them to do the work God designed them to do. Take Joseph, for example. Genesis 41:38–40 says,

> *So Pharaoh asked them, "Can we find anyone like this man, one in whom is the Spirit of God?" Then Pharaoh said to Joseph, "Since God has made all this known to you, there is no one so discerning and wise as you. You shall be in charge of my palace, and all my people are to submit to your orders. Only with respect to the throne will I be greater than you."*

Because the Holy Spirit enabled Joseph to interpret visions and dreams, Joseph was given the position of leadership in Egypt.

Later on we read Joshua is chosen to replace Moses as Israel's leader. Numbers 27:18 (NKJV) describes him as *a man in whom is the Spirit*, a necessary quality for leadership.

Judges 6:34 tells how the Spirit of the Lord came on Gideon, enabling him to lead people into victory. Judges 13–16 makes it clear Samson was led by the Spirit of the Lord and all of his power came directly from the Holy Spirit.

Later, in 1 Samuel 10–11 we read that the Holy Spirit came on Saul after he was chosen to be king of Israel, enabling him to prophecy and go to war to defend the people of Israel. However, in 1 Samuel 16:14 we read that the Holy Spirit departed from him because of his disobedience.

In 1 Samuel 16:13 we read about Samuel anointing David king. So Samuel took the horn of oil and anointed him in the presence of his brothers, and from that day on the Spirit of the Lord came powerfully upon David.

In Numbers 24:2 the Spirit of God caused Balaam to prophesy good things for Israel when he was hired to curse them.

As we move into the New Testament, the Holy Spirit is right there at the nativity. Luke 1 tells the story of the angel Gabriel telling the virgin Mary that she would give birth to the Messiah. When she asked "How?" the answer was, *The Holy Spirit will come on you, and the power of the Most High will overshadow you. So the holy one to be born will be called the Son of God.*

Later, in Luke 1:67, we read that Zechariah was filled with the Holy Spirit and prophesied.

After the extraordinary display of the Trinity during Jesus's baptism, Luke 4:1 says, *Jesus, full of the Holy Spirit, left the Jordan and was led by the Spirit into the wilderness.* When his time of temptation in the wilderness was over, Luke 4:14 says, *Jesus returned to Galilee in the power of the Spirit, and news about him spread through the whole countryside.* He was teaching in their synagogues, and everyone praised him.

As we continue to read the Gospels, we see Jesus ministering to people. We read of him teaching, healing the sick, casting out demons, and raising the dead. When the Pharisees accused him of casting out demons using Satan's power, Jesus replied that he casts out demons by the power of the Holy Spirit (Matthew 12:28–29 and Luke 11:20)

In John 14, Jesus began teaching his disciples about the Holy Spirit. He knew the time for him to be crucified was quickly approaching, and he wanted them to know that even after he was gone they would not be alone. John 14:16 says, *And I will ask the Father, and he will give you another advocate to help you and be with you forever.*

Even though Jesus knew his time on earth was coming to an end, he gave his disciples the promise of the Holy Spirit to guide them throughout their lives and their ministry. After his death and resurrection, just before he ascended into heaven, his final instructions to them were to go to Jerusalem and wait for the Holy Spirit.

"Do not leave Jerusalem, but wait for the my Father promised, which you have heard me speak about. For John baptized with water, but in a few days you will be baptized with the Holy Spirit." (Acts 1:4–5)

Act 2:1–4 tells about the arrival of the Holy Spirit in the early church.

When the day of Pentecost came, they were all together in one place. Suddenly a sound like the blowing of a violent wind came from heaven and filled the whole house where they were sitting. They saw what seemed to be tongues of fire that separated and came to rest on each of them. All of them were filled with the Holy Spirit and began to speak in other tongues as the Spirit enabled them.

This was only the beginning of the work of the Holy Spirit in the lives of the early church. If you continue to read through the book of Acts, you will see the Holy Spirit anointing people to preach and share the good news of Jesus Christ. Frequently, their words were accompanied by signs and wonders (Acts 6:8–10). Through the power of the Holy Spirit people prophesied (Acts 11:28, Acts 19:6), healed the sick (Acts 19:11–12), raised the dead (Acts 9), and cast out demons (Acts 16:18). As Jesus promised, the Holy Spirit gave them the right words to speak when they were questioned by authorities and the strength to endure persecution with joy and forgiveness (Acts 7:55, Acts 20:23). Following the leading of the Holy Spirit, the early church carried the gospel of Jesus throughout the ancient world.

You're probably thinking, "Wow, Jamie, that was a lot of Scripture!" I know it seems like a lot, but I wanted to prove a point: **whenever God did an amazing work or a great thing, it was through the power of the Holy Spirit working in and through the lives of ordinary, average men.** The same is still true today!

The good news for us is the powerful work of the Holy Spirit didn't end at the close of New Testament times. The same Holy Spirit who was present at creation, worked throughout the Old Testament, filled Jesus, and anointed and guided the early church wants to be equally active in our lives today. Allowing him to play a living, vibrant, active role in your day-to-day life is the key to living a Spirit-led life.

Let's look a few of the ways the Holy Spirit wants to actively influence your life.

1. THE HOLY SPIRIT CONVICTS US OF SIN

When He [the Holy Spirit] has come, He will convict the world of sin, and of righteousness, and of judgment (John 16:8 NKJV).

One of the Holy Spirit's main functions is convicting people of sin in their lives. Rather than seeing this as a bad thing, Christians need to see this as an exciting opportunity to change, become more Christ-like, and deepen their relationship with God. The truth is that all of us have different areas we need to overcome and replace sinful patterns with God's ways. We are all in the process of separating from sin and evil and dedicating ourselves to the worship and service of Christ. This process is called sanctification.

When the Holy Spirit convicts us of sin, he is challenging us to take another step forward in this process. Conviction says, "This sin is providing an obstacle in your relationship with God and a barrier to you becoming all God wants you to be. It's time to repent, abandon this sin, and form a new behavioral pattern following the principles of the Bible."

Conviction is like a WRONG WAY sign. Its sole purpose is to make you aware that you are going in the wrong direction so you can turn around and get back on course. The benefit of living a Spirit-led life and heeding the Holy Spirit's voice of conviction is that he will make you aware of the sin in your life so you can make adjustments and get on the right spiritual path.

For example, remember the story I told you in the beginning of this chapter about not e-mailing my friend? It was the Holy Spirit who convicted my heart to show me that I had sinned by not obeying his voice. This conviction caused me to repent, readjust my course, and learn the necessity of obeying when God tells me to do something.

Heeding the voice of the Holy Spirit when he convicts you of sin should be an ongoing process in the life of every believer. It is our duty to keep our spiritual ears open and our hearts sensitive so we can experience the conviction of the Holy Spirit, and quickly respond in repentance and change. As we grow closer to God and live a more Spirit-led life, sensing and responding to the conviction of the Holy Spirit will become a common occurrence as he leads you into a holier, more sanctified, more intimate relationship with Jesus. What an awesome gift!

2. THE HOLY SPIRIT GUIDES US INTO ALL TRUTH

But when he, the Spirit of truth, comes, he will guide you into all truth (John 16:13).

We live in a world where it is hard to know what is true and what is false. Deception runs rampant through families, through society, and sometimes even throughout the church. How can a Christian know what is true and what is a lie? The answer is by relying on the Holy Spirit. One way the Holy Spirit leads us into truth is by giving us the gift of discernment. Using this spiritual gift, we will be able to judge right from wrong, truth from lies, and the things of God versus cheap imitations.

Another common way the Holy Spirit leads us into truth is by helping us to better understand the Bible and apply it to our own lives. Under his guidance, the words of the Bible become a living Word for each of us. As we study the teachings of Jesus, the Holy Spirit gives us insight into their meanings. The NIV Disciple Study Bible says John 16:13 this way, *The Spirit is present at the Christian's study desk and in every Christian study group, leading believers into all truth.*

3. THE HOLY SPIRIT CONSUMES US

This is commonly known as being baptized with the Holy Spirit. The initial physical evidence, or the receipt giving us confirmation, is speaking in tongues. Many say, "Why do I need to be baptized in the Holy Spirit? Doesn't the Holy Spirit fill me at salvation?"

The answer to this question is yes and no. When we get saved, we begin to experience the Holy Spirit's influence and convicting power. However, the baptism in the Holy Spirit is a separate thing. The Bible teaches us that the baptism of the Holy Spirit is a special experience following salvation, but separate from salvation. It's when the power of the Holy Spirit consumes our lives, filling us with power to witness to others.

Let me explain what I mean. One way to think about this is to think about chocolate milk. Have you ever made chocolate milk? Chocolate milk is one of my favorite things to drink for breakfast. When you make chocolate milk, you start with a glass of plain white milk. The glass of milk represents us as believers.

Then you grab your chocolate syrup and you pour it into the glass. The chocolate syrup represents the Holy Spirit. When we get saved, the Holy Spirit comes and lives inside us. As anyone who ever made chocolate milk knows, when you pour the chocolate into the milk, the milk starts to change a little. You notice the brown syrup peeking through the white liquid. This is like how the Holy Spirit helps us change by convicting us of sin.

The final ingredient to making chocolate milk is a spoon. The spoon represents the baptism of the Holy Spirit. Basically, the baptism of the Holy Spirit gives us power. As we serve God and work for him, it is the equivalent of a spoon stirring the glass of milk. As the power, or the spoon, stirs, you cannot see the brown chocolate or the white milk. They are now one, working together.

The power of the spoon is changing the milk and making it even better than it was before it was filled. We are no longer separate from the Holy Spirit. The Holy Spirit, represented by the chocolate syrup, is flowing through us and consuming us. The Holy Spirit takes over and uses us to reach the lost. We function and serve under his power, not our own strength.

I hope this word picture helped you see why we need to be baptized in the Holy Spirit. We need the Holy Spirit to convict us and help us. But we especially need the power of the Holy Spirit to consume us and flow through us so we can reach the lost. So I encourage you to start pursuing the baptism in the Holy Spirit. Being filled with the Holy Spirit is a huge part of men putting on godly manhood.

4. THE HOLY SPIRIT GUIDES BELIEVERS

As Christians, our number one goal in life should be knowing and living in God's will. The question is, how can Christians know which direction God wants them to go and what he wants them to do? The answer is living a life that is led by the Holy Spirit.

Acts 20:22–24 records Paul's statements to the Ephesian elders, explaining how he knew it was God's will for him to go to Jerusalem.

And now, compelled by the Spirit, I am going to Jerusalem, not knowing what will happen to me there. I only know that in every city the Holy Spirit warns me that prison and hardships are facing me. However, I consider my life worth nothing to me; my only aim is to finish the race and complete the task the Lord Jesus has given me—the task of testifying to the good news of God's grace.

Just as Paul knew God's will because of the guidance of the Holy Spirit, Christians today can learn God's will through the guidance of the Holy Spirit. Romans 8:14 says, *For those who are led by the Spirit of God are the children of God.*

The same Holy Spirit that told Paul to go to Jerusalem wants to direct your steps everyday of your life. He wants to be *your* guide, the GPS for *your* life. He wants to develop a relationship with you that allows him to speak to your heart and give you direction.

The story I told at the beginning of the chapter was an example of this point. The Holy Spirit was guiding me and telling me how he wanted me to touch someone else's life. It is God's will that this be commonplace in the lives of all believers—that we be guided by the Holy Spirit to accomplish the will and the work of God on earth.

You see, as with all parts of Christianity, there are two sides of the coin. On the one hand, there is the tremendous gift God has offered us. In this case, we are specifically talking about the opportunity to lead a Spirit-led life. On the other hand, we have our response. Am I willing to live *my* life guided by the Holy Spirit?

At the beginning of this chapter, I shared the story of the Holy Spirit offering me the opportunity to help someone. I chose not to seize the moment and listen to his voice. What kept me from following him? Business? Maybe doubt? In the end, whatever excuses kept me from obeying his voice didn't matter. When he allowed me to see that it was him speaking to me to meet someone's genuine need, my heart was broken.

Mostly, I was heartbroken because I truly love God and I want to walk in step with every plan he has for my life—no matter how big or small. This incident revived a fresh passion inside of me that says, "I want to follow you, no matter how big, how small, how difficult or how easy the task. I want to live a Spirit-led life."

> **Our heart's desire needs to be a desire to experience the freedom that comes from living in the Holy Spirit's truth.**

This prayer has extended beyond simply choosing that I will always obey what I feel the Holy Spirit is speaking to my heart. It carries over into a desire to embrace the Spirit's work of convicting of sin. If something I am doing, saying, watching on television, listening to on the radio, wearing, or even thinking grieves the Holy Spirit in any way, then I want my heart to be tender enough to sense his conviction. When I feel his conviction, I want to quickly repent and quickly change my course.

I want the Holy Spirit to guide me into all truth. I want to grow in my understanding of God's Word and how it can be applied to my life. No longer do I want to rely on my own vision and rationale to understand people and situations, but I want to see through spiritual eyes. I want to see what is really true and respond accordingly. The Bible says, *Then you will know the truth, and the truth will set you free* (John 8:32). It's my heart's desire to experience the freedom that comes from living in the Holy Spirit's truth.

This experience whet my appetite to hear the Holy Spirit's voice guide each step in my life. It was encouraging to know I wasn't just dreaming up ideas, but the Holy Spirit actually was speaking to me. This episode is giving me the bravery and the courage to step out of the proverbial boat and take the risk of following the Holy Spirit's leading. It taught me that even if I fall, I'd rather err on the side of obedience and faith than play it safe and sit in the boat, wondering what would have happened while the winds of the Spirit pass me by. I'm excited about the possibilities. As I write, I pray this excitement will be contagious, and you too will commit yourself to taking the risk of leading a Spirit-led life.

Christians often say, "Wouldn't it be great if we had lived in New Testament times? After all, they walked and talked with Jesus. They saw miracles. The gospel spread like a wildfire. If only we'd lived back then." As we long for the Spirit-led lives of the early disciples, we don't even realize there is no need for nostalgia. It is available to us right now, today!

The same Holy Spirit that raised Christ from the dead dwells in you (Romans 8:11)! He wants you to live the same dynamic, Spirit-filled life as the believers in New Testament times. Just like he did with them, he wants to be your GPS for life saying, "Go here. Go there. Minister to this person. Speak a word to this person. Repent of this sin. Change this behavior. Don't believe that lie; this is the truth." He desires to have a living, active, functioning role in your life.

The question is, will you allow him?

Will you put away your childish way of relying on yourself for guidance, direction, and strength? Will you put on manhood and make the choice and commitment to live a Spirit-led life? Will you obey the Holy Spirit's voice when he speaks to you?

When he convicts you of sin, will you quickly repent and change?

Do you want to see real truth? Are you open to abandoning lies? Are you willing to take a chance and obey his voice even when it doesn't make sense? Do you want to live a Spirit-filled life? The opportunity is there, the choice is yours.

GROUP STUDY QUESTIONS

1. What is something you learned about the Holy Spirit that you didn't know before?

2. Have there been times in your life when you ignored the direction of the Holy Spirit? What was the result?

3. In what ways has the Holy Spirit convicted you of sin in your life?

4. How does the Holy Spirit aid you in your Bible reading?

5. Have you experienced the baptism in the Holy Spirit? Describe this experience.

6. Do you allow the Holy Spirit to guide your daily life?

7. How can we as a group help you live a Spirit-led life?

SECTION III

LIVING A LIFE
WORTHY
OF THE CALLING

·8·

WHAT YOU SPEND SHOWS WHO YOU ARE

In Section Three of this book, we're going to look at how, in order to put on manhood, we need to live a life worthy of the calling. What exactly does this phrase mean? Allow me to use an example to explain.

In the movie *The Blind Side*, which was based on a true story, Michael Oher was a young man who had absolutely nothing. He had no home, no family, no education, only the clothes on his back. He was even going without food because he had no money to buy it. He had nothing—not even hope. If no one intervened in his situation, he would be destined to a life of poverty, crime, and very likely the most probable fate for a young man like him was an early, unnecessary death.

But then someone intervened. A neighbor pulled a lot of strings and got him into a private school. But even this didn't solve his problem. Then he met the Touhy family—specifically Leigh Ann Touhy. They rescued him. They essentially "adopted" him into their family and treated him just like they treated their own children. Now he didn't just have a place to stay, he had a room of his own designed for his own needs. He had plenty of food, clothes, and they even bought him a car.

While all of these material possessions were great, the best thing they gave him was a loving family. He wasn't seen as their house guest. He was treated like family. So much so that when they asked him if he wanted them to adopt him and make him part of the family, he said, "I thought I already was."

They gave him love, emotional support, and helped him deal with his issues. They gave him everything he needed to succeed in life, to overcome his learning issues, and even hired a tutor. Joining their family completely changed his life. He went from having nothing to having everything; most importantly, a family.

As Michael was in his senior year in high school he had to pick which college he wanted to go to. There was a whole controversy with the NCAA, resulting in him having to answer why he wanted to go to the University of Mississippi. He answered, "Because my family went there— I want to carry on the traditions, follow in the footsteps of my new family." Ephesians 4:1 says a similar thought, *As a prisoner for the Lord, then, I urge you to live a life worthy of the calling you have received.*

"Live a life worthy of the calling you have received."

You have to understand what Paul is talking about here. In chapters 1–3, Paul talks about our spiritual condition before Christ broke down the barrier and made a way for us to be saved.

Spiritually we had nothing. Most of all, we had no hope. We were as spiritually poverty stricken and hopeless as Michael Oher was physically. *But then,* Christ came and died on the cross. He not only reconciled man to God, but through his death on the cross, he broke down the barrier that kept us from having any access to God's kingdom, his promises, his covenant, and his community.

But then, Christ intervened. Now we are adopted in God's kingdom and given the full rights, full access, full equality. We are offered a new life filled with everything God has to offer—particularly a personal, intimate relationship with him. Like Michael Oher, we've gone from having *nothing* to having the full rights as God's children.

It is now our responsibility to live a life worthy of this calling. How do we do this? Over the next few chapters, we will be looking at various ways to live a life worthy of the calling. We're going to get started in this chapter by examining how a man who is leaving his childish ways and putting on manhood needs to be a man who is financially responsible.

Money? Why are we talking about money in a book about growing spiritually? Is it really necessary to talk finances when learning how to grow in your walk with God?

Of course it is! Why? Because how you spend your money shows who you are. Think about the topics we have discussed so far. The Bible says if you live in debt, you are slave to the debt and the person to whom you owe. So if you are in debt to someone else, it will affect your ability to follow God wholeheartedly like we discussed in Chapter Two.

In Chapter Three we discussed the need to get our priorities straight. Money is a huge part of priorities because what you spend your money on is what is important to you.

In Chapter Four, we looked at the need to be devoted to your church. This includes devoting your money, rather, God's money that he lets you have, to the church. Tithing and giving are both spiritual and financial issues.

In Chapter Five we discussed the need to be accountable. This also applies to finances. Financial accountability and stewardship are huge issues we all need to face.

In the last chapter, we looked at the need to live a Spirit-led life. This is especially true when it comes to our finances. The Holy Spirit should be an active participant in our finances, showing us how to spend our money and how to budget.

I truly believe a man who is putting on manhood must make changes to his financial life and money management. So that's what we're going to discuss in this chapter.

The first area to examine is the need to show our thanks to God for allowing us to spend his money. Does that sound like an odd way to word the sentence? After all, we work hard and earn our money. But the reality of the situation is that God allows us to earn the money. He supplies the job, and he expects us to be a good steward of the money. Part of being a good steward is doing something called *tithing*.

Tithing is when we give back to God ten percent of the money he gives us, via our local church. It's God's will for all men to give ten percent of our paycheck, and not the leftover part. We give God ten percent before the government helps themselves to some.

Sounds like a drag, right? After all, times are tough, people are struggling, and we need every dollar we have. Why do we have to give ten percent back to God?

Because he said to do it! There is no better reason, and there should really be no argument. We should gratefully give it to God, realizing he blesses us by allowing us to keep the other ninety percent.

You may be thinking, "I get it—we need to tithe—our pastor tells us this all the time. But I want to learn how to grow closer to God and have his hand of blessing on my life and my finances."

My answer to you is simple. If you want the blessing of God on your life and finances, you have to tithe. If you don't tithe to him, he won't bless you.

No man can expect to grow and prosper in God's kingdom if he isn't tithing. Why? Because the Bible says that a man who doesn't tithe is a man who is stealing from God. Malachi 3:8–10 says,

> *Will a mere mortal rob God? Yet you rob me.*
>
> *But you ask, "How are we robbing you?"*
>
> *In tithes and offerings. You are under a curse—your whole nation—because you are robbing me. Bring the whole tithe into the storehouse, that there may be food in my house. Test me in this, says the LORD Almighty, and see if I will not throw open the floodgates of heaven and pour out so much blessing that there will not be room enough to store it.*

Do we really think God is going to bless us and grow us spiritually if we are stealing from him? Yet, it clearly says you steal from God when you don't tithe. God even says he can't bless you, and he offers a challenge to try tithing and see if he doesn't prosper you.

So men need to be faithful and give God ten percent of our money, and we need to do it happily, thanking him that he provided us with the other ninety percent. Seriously, a man of God cannot afford not to tithe.

Tithing isn't the only area of finances we need to look at if we are going to move from living in our childish ways and begin to put on godly manhood. God not only wants men to give him back ten percent, but he also wants us to be good stewards over the other ninety percent he allows us to keep. God doesn't ask it, he demands it!

The number one way to ensure we are good stewards of God's money is to live on a budget. A budget keeps us focused on how we spend the money and it helps us avoid debt.

Every man, whatever your age or economic level, needs to live on a budget. A budget is a plan. It tells you how much money you have and where it must go. It provides boundaries for how much can be spent in an area. It also provides freedom, because you know when you need something, the money is there.

Living without a budget is like trying to build a house without blueprints. You can't keep adding stairways, pipes, or wires without knowing how much of each is needed and where it is going. In both cases, you'll end up with the same result—*a big mess.* Living on a budget avoids the big mess. It gives you a plan to follow to avoid financial destruction. It is an absolute necessity.

A lot of guys freak at the word "budget." They can't imagine living with a structured financial system that doesn't allow you to buy what you want when you want it and letting it all ride on the credit card. The structure and confines of a budget seem so restricting.

However, it's the exact opposite. Rather than being restrictive and oppressive, a budget is actually freeing. Knowing there is enough money to pay all the bills when they are due releases enormous money stress. The boundaries a budget provides let you know how much you can spend. If you stay within the restraints of the budget, you can live without the pressure of consumer debt. It is great!

Whether you are a teenager with an allowance or a job, or a college student learning to live within your means while balancing tuition, rent, car payments, and living expenses, a father managing a family budget, or even a grandpa enjoying your retirement, you need to budget your money. Many money pitfalls can be avoided by living on a budget.

This chapter of our book is meant to open our eyes to the need to be financially responsible. We are not going to go in-depth of how to set up a budget or manage your finances, but if you would like more information on this topic, download our free ebook, *Money Lessons 101*, at **www. mantourministries.com**. It's a great resource my sister and I have put together to help people work on getting their financial house in order. It shows how God took our family from the brink of financial ruin and helped us get out of debt and live according to his financial principles.

But for now, I just want to show you how a man who is putting on manhood will work on living a financially responsible life. He will understand his responsibility to God to give back ten percent, he will be grateful to God he gets to keep the other ninety percent, and he will live on a budget and avoid living in huge amounts of debt. But that's not all. In order to be able to do any of this, you must learn to curb your appetites.

This is a huge part of putting on manhood. Why? Because if you are using your money to meet every want and desire you have, you're acting like a child. If you use money to meet your inner needs or to make you feel like a big man, you are behaving childishly. If you use money to buy friends or gain the esteem of others, you're acting like a kid. If you are racking up huge amounts of consumer debt, you are not handling money in a grown-up manner. So failure to manage your finances equals staying in your childish ways, and this is not the goal we are striving to obtain.

To stop this behavior and put on manhood, we need to get to the root of the problem: our appetites.

It's like a child who has a dollar burning a hole in his pocket. Through some series of circumstances, like Grandma sending a card, or completing a list of chores, this little one got his hands on some money. Instantly, he couldn't wait to spend it! There were so many delightful things in the world that could belong to him if only he could get Mom and Dad to take him to the store. And waiting isn't an option—he wants to go and spend his dollar *now*!

Last year one of the little girls in my Junior Bible Quiz received a check from her Grandma a few weeks before Christmas. That afternoon, she was going to the toy store to "Christmas shop" (although I'm not sure which of her older brothers and sisters wanted a gift from Toys"R"Us). She could hardly sit still during class because she was so excited about going and spending her money. It was adorable!

The funny thing is sometimes behaviors that seem adorable on children are very unattractive on adults. It isn't cute to see an adult have this same childish attitude toward money. Maybe that's because "childish" actions are expected of children, but unacceptable in adults.

That's why we need to look at finances as we endeavor to put on manhood. There comes a point in every person's life when he or she needs to put aside immature money management habits and begin approaching finances from the perspective of a mature adult. We have already discussed tithing and the need to live on a budget. While this is vital, it is not all there is to it.

We have to learn to curb our appetites for things. One of the biggest challenges is moving past our need for instant gratification and beginning to wisely manage and save our money. We do this by learning to curb our appetites.

Ultimately, it's the appetites in our souls that cause us to spend money rather than save it. Until we deal with the deficiencies causing our appetites, we'll never be able to overcome the problem of deficient funds in our savings accounts and living on a budget.

Let's start by defining what I mean by the word *appetite*.

An appetite is a craving of the soul that has never been satisfied. It is striving after or toward something. It is something yearned for or longed for that is never filled or satisfied. We use a variety of things and ways to fill this craving.

> **A budget is actually freeing. Knowing there is enough money to pay all the bills when they are due releases enormous money stress.**

Appetites operate from our soul, the seat of our emotions, then through the heart and mind. They consume as much of the mind as they can. We want and want but nothing satisfies. So we buy and buy and end up in debt.

Solomon describes it this way in Ecclesiastes 6:7, *Everyone's toil is for their mouth, yet their appetite is never satisfied.*

What causes us to have appetites?

Some people have appetites from deep needs in the soul that were never met. They think filling their appetites through instant gratification will fill their emotional needs.

Some appetites come from trying to prove to someone else we are better than he or she is. This can consume our lives, causing the tendency to become a workaholic.

Some allow appetites to take the place of God. Things are used to fill the void only God can fill.

Some have appetites as adults because they grew up poor and resolved to never be poor again. So they work more and more to buy more and more. They live extravagantly and usually in debt. There are all kinds of unfulfilled needs each of us has in our souls, because we live in an imperfect world and were raised by imperfect people. This is all a part of life.

I know in my life it was a mixture of these reasons. As a child, I was always told we couldn't afford to live like everyone else, so I decided in my heart that when I was older and had money of my own, I would never do without the things everyone else had. I also spent money to make myself feel like a big man, easing the feelings of inadequacy I faced because of physical disabilities. I used money to buy things to ease the pain of years of undealt-with abuse.

All this is to say I used money to meet my emotional needs deep inside, and, as a result, I didn't handle money maturely or responsibly. Instead, I was bound and chained to my childish ways. I had to face my childish ways and let the Holy Spirit teach me how to handle money properly. He did this by making me begin facing my appetites.

Appetites, no matter their origin in our soul, want us to entertain the flesh by keeping busy, keeping occupied with the things in the world, doing all kinds of activities, working, overeating, shopping, living for sports, and worshipping the body. They make the flesh desire happiness and we will do whatever it takes to make our flesh happy. In today's world, all these activities and things eat up our money. So we spend and live beyond our budgets to live in a state of debt.

Can you see why we need to address the issue of our appetites in order to be able to budget money and live financially responsible lives? Realistically, the reason Americans are struggling financially isn't simply a *financial* problem. Even in this time of recession, our incomes are still among the highest in the world. The reason Americans struggle is that our lifestyle expectations and our emotional appetites are controlling our lives rather than our common sense.

We spend money we don't have to fill our emotional needs when what we should be doing is allowing God to heal and fill our emotional needs, and we should be using common sense to manage our money. One of the keys to getting your financial house in order is first realizing how your emotional needs and appetites are affecting your spending habits.

How do we do this?

First, we start with prayer. We need to ask the Holy Spirit to show us what our appetites are and what emotional needs those appetites are trying to fill. Sometimes we have to look at the lives of our parents, grand-parents, great-grandparents and see what they lived for and what made them happy.

What made them feel good, successful? How did they spend their money?

What did they do with their time?

We grew up watching them and we imitate their behavior and practices. God has to cleanse us from repeating their sinful ways and wrong uses of money and develop his ways in us. Learning from the past is very valuable. You can see what needs changing inside you and the direction God needs to take you.

> **We spend money we don't have to fill our emotional needs, when what we should be doing is allowing God to heal and fill our emotional needs and using common sense to manage our money.**

Another question to ask yourself is, how did my past affect my life?

Did your parents meet your emotional needs or leave an empty void inside?

Did you have physical restraints that didn't allow you to be like all the other kids?

Were you poor growing up and others made fun of you? Appetites can drive us to buy things we think we missed growing up. We convince ourselves we need them.

After you've looked at your past, you need to look at your present. Ask yourself some questions like: What are my appetites? What do I live for? What consumes my time? What do I have desires for in life? Are they for God? This world? Money? Clothes? Sports? TV? Cars? What? What do I hunger and thirst for deep inside my soul?

What do I set my eyes on?

What does my heart lust after? What do I spend my time on?

How much of this world do I crave and participate in?

Once we know the answers to these questions, we will start to recognize our appetites—the emotional issues screaming, "Feed me, or I'll die!"

The next question is, how do we change? How do we get rid of our appetites?

First, you need to recognize your specific appetites and what you do to fill them. Do you shop when you're sad? Do you spend money when you're bored? Do you buy new expensive "toys" you can't afford because you're lonely? Are you trying to buy your wife's or your children's love? The first step to overcoming is recognizing how your appetites affect your behavior.

Next, you need to confess your appetites to God. Proverbs 28:13 says, *Whoever conceals their sins does not prosper, but the one who confesses and renounces them finds mercy.*

Ask God to forgive you. Ask him to forgive you for putting your cravings first in your life before him.

Renounce any control you have given to the oppression of a demon of "appetites" in your life. Demons are very real, and while they cannot posses a Christian because we are filled with the Holy Spirit, they certainly do their best to oppress us and trap us into

> **Appetites consume as much of the mind as they can. We want and want but nothing satisfies. So we buy and buy and end up in debt.**

their way of thinking and acting. We can't tolerate it in our lives. (If you want to learn more about this topic of demonic oppression, I highly recommend the book *Fight* by Kenny Luck). In the name of Jesus and through his blood, reclaim the fact that you are a child of God and no demonic influence can affect you any longer. Then, you will be free of this demonic oppression to follow Jesus. By doing this, the struggle to overcome will be a little easier. It won't totally solve the problem, because we made grooves in our brains through our behavior and actions, but it will take the demonic oppression away. This enables the Holy Spirit's power to change us, lead us, and guide us.

Then comes the practical part. Change your mind and lifestyle by reading the Bible and obeying what it says. Ask God to lead you in your new financial journey to freedom. This is the prayer of a man pursuing God, not a boy stuck in his childish ways, and it is a prayer God will answer because it lines up with his will!

God longs for his sons to be faithful with their finances. He wants men who appreciate the many blessings he gives them and who show this appreciation through tithing and being good stewards of the rest. He loves it when his sons use money to meet their physical needs instead of using money to meet their emotional needs and longings. This is a man living a life worthy of the calling!

GROUP STUDY QUESTIONS

1. Why is financial responsibility vital to putting on manhood?

2. Do you tithe? If so, why? If not, why not?

3. What does it mean to be a good steward of the remaining ninety percent?

4. What are some reasons for living on a budget? Do you live on a budget?

5. How do our appetites affect our finances?

6. What is an appetite you have to guard against in order to handle money like a godly man?

7. How can we as a group help you apply the lessons in this chapter?

·9·

WHO LET THE DOGS OUT?

Usually when I write, I like to begin by painting a word picture or using a good example to grab your attention. However, in this chapter, we aren't going to have a funny anecdote or an attention-grabbing story to start the chapter. We have a serious subject to look at, so we are going to dive into it head first.

In order to put on manhood, a man of God needs to act like a man and not a dog with women! How's that for a blunt statement? It sounds crude and harsh, but it's a truth God's men need to hear.

God's men cannot treat women like objects or ways to meet our needs and desires. To do so is to stay stuck in our childish ways. A man who is going to leave his childish ways behind him and put on manhood is going to treat women as they really are, precious daughters of our heavenly Father. Unfortunately, the opposite seems to be the trend in society, and God's men are falling into these traps all around us.

Recently, I read a statistic that at first surprised me. It stated nine out of ten men said sexual temptation and sin was the main thing that keeps them from a deep, meaningful relationship with God. While at first I was surprised by this number, upon further thought, I realized it was probably true. After all, sexual thoughts and temptations are one of Satan's most-used plays in his centuries-old playbook to destroy God's men. For years, he has used sexual temptations to sink many men.

In this chapter, we'll learn how to change our way of thinking so we won't be hit so hard with this particular attack. It's time to put away our childish ways when it comes to women and sex, and start living a life worthy of the calling we have received!

Let's face it: because of the moral depravity and extreme level of sexual material constantly available to us through many different media outlets, our minds have become tainted and contaminated. They are no longer as pure as they should be. Our sinful minds have learned many degrading thought patterns which need to change.

Together we must learn new ways to think and feel about sexual temptation so we can live a life worthy of this great calling we have received. To do this, we'll look at one of my favorite books of the Bible. In the book of Joshua we'll study the story of two spies who demonstrate to us the proper way to think and act toward women.

I have always loved a good spy mystery. Unfortunately, these types of spy movies and TV shows often contribute to the problem we're discussing as Hollywood spies tend to degrade and use women. However, there are good examples of spies we can look to in life. We are going to examine such men. As we turn to Joshua 2, we see the story of two daring spies on a life-or-death mission.

Allow me to set the stage. After forty years of wandering in the wilderness, the children of Israel are getting ready to begin their conquest of their Promised Land. Joshua, the leader of the Israelites, wanted to begin the attack of the Promised Land. Before the battle could begin, he needed some espionage work done in verse 1 (NKJV):

Now Joshua the son of Nun sent out two men from Acacia Grove to spy secretly, saying, "Go, view the land, especially Jericho."

You can almost hear the familiar *Mission Impossible* music blaring in the background and Joshua saying to the two men, "Your mission, should you choose to accept it, is to go into the land of Canaan and survey the land. Look it over. Check out the people. Check out the geography, the weak and strong points. Check out the military and the fortification. Bring back this information and any evidence to back it up." You almost wonder if there was a tape that self-destructed.

As we return to Joshua 2, it appears the two spies' mission went relatively well. However, this changed when they entered the city of Jericho.

> *So they went, and came to the house of a harlot named Rahab, and lodged there. And it was told the king of Jericho, saying, "Behold, men have come here tonight from the children of Israel to search out the country."*

> *So the king of Jericho sent to Rahab, saying, "Bring out the men who have come to you, who have entered your house, for they have come to search out all the country."*

> *Then the woman took the two men and hid them. So she said, "Yes, the men came to me, but I did not know where they were from. And it happened as the gate was being shut, when it was dark, that the men went out. Where the men went I do not know; pursue them quickly, for you may overtake them." (But she had brought them up to the roof and hidden them with the stalks of flax, which she had laid in order on the roof.)*

> *Then the men pursued them by the road to the Jordan, to the fords. And as soon as those who pursued them had gone out, they shut the gate.*

The two spies' secret mission was discovered. They were exposed and in immediate danger! To remain safe, they took refuge in the home of a woman named Rahab.

Rahab helped the two men by hiding them and lying about their whereabouts. Once the soldiers who were searching for the spies were diverted away from her house, we read that Rahab went up to the roof to see the men.

How many times has Hollywood used this plot in their spy movies? We all know what would have happened next in a movie as the secret agents are hidden overnight by a woman, especially one deemed a prostitute in verse one. However, this thinking is exactly the type of groove which needs to be replaced in our heads. Our minds should not naturally go there!

We cannot have our minds, which are supposed to be becoming holy like Jesus's, automatically degrade women and treat them as sexual objects. We must become men who see women as holy vessels and spiritual beings that should be loved, honored, respected, and protected. This is exactly how we see these two spies treat Rahab. Their example shows us how we should treat all women as we endeavor to live a life worthy of the calling.

1. WE NEED TO TRUST WOMEN, NOT USE THEM.

The first attitude we see these men display toward Rahab was one of trust. The text does not indicate that the two men had any idea who Rahab was or how she would treat them. However, instead of looking at her as a dishonest woman, they decided to put their lives in her hands.

That is trust. They didn't let her occupation deter them. They didn't see her as a prostitute. They saw her as a person they could depend upon.

While on earth, Jesus was the model of a man who trusted women. When Jesus's mother came to him begging him to help the wine situation at a wedding at Cana, he trusted her opinion and did what she asked. We read in the Gospels that Jesus entrusted his well-being to a group of women who supported him financially. Jesus trusted Mary Magdalene to go tell his disciples he had risen from the dead. Jesus regularly placed his trust in women and we need to do the same.

2. WE MUST TREAT WOMEN WITH DIGNITY, NOT DISGRACE.

The second thing to notice about the two spies' treatment of Rahab was they treated her with dignity and respect. Rahab was a woman with a shady past and a bad reputation. She was not a pillar of virtue. However, these two men overlooked this and showed her nothing but dignity and respect. They listened to what she said. They didn't degrade her or look down on her. They were courteous, kind, and respectful.

This is one area where we as men must grow and mature. God wants his men to treat all women with dignity and respect. We need to honor them. It's the way Jesus treated women. Nowhere in the Bible will you ever find Jesus being disrespectful or condescending to women. It never happened. We need to come to the place where we see any disrespect or degradation of women as sin. Like these two spies, we must be respectful with all women no matter who they are or what they have done.

3. WE MUST VALUE THE THOUGHTS AND OPINIONS OF WOMEN.

The third thing to notice is the two spies valued Rahab's thoughts and opinions.

> *Now before they lay down, she came up to them on the roof, and said to the men: "I know that the LORD has given you the land, that the terror of you has fallen on us, and that all the inhabitants of the land are fainthearted because of you. For we have heard how the LORD dried up the water of the Red Sea for you when you came out of Egypt, and what you did to the two kings of the Amorites who were on the other side of the Jordan, Sihon and Og, whom you utterly destroyed. And as soon as we heard these things, our hearts melted; neither did there remain any more courage in anyone because of you, for the LORD your God, He is God in heaven above and on earth beneath.*

107

We read here that Rahab told the two spies what she thought about the Israelites' battle plans. She told them about the morale among the people of Jericho; they were scared to death. She shared what she thought their chances of victory would be. To see the men's response, we must skip ahead to the end of the chapter.

And they said to Joshua, "Truly the LORD has delivered all the land into our hands, for indeed all the inhabitants of the country are fainthearted because of us."

They essentially told Joshua just what Rahab told them. They repeated her opinions. They listened to her. They heard her point of view. They took her seriously. They worked with her in order to accomplish their mission. They didn't see her as inferior. They didn't look down on her for having strong opinions. They didn't feel they were smarter. They listened, learned, and followed what she said.

We must learn this lesson from the two spies. In the book of Genesis, we read God created Eve because Adam needed a helpmate. He was incomplete without her.

Men and women think differently. Men think in a linear manner...A to B to C. Women have a greater ability than men to think more emotionally and see the entire picture. We need women to give us a different and sometimes better perspective. Unfortunately, Hollywood and the pornography industry portray women as unintelligent people who are only for sexual pleasure. Nothing could be further from the truth.

Women have the ability to see things in a situation a man would never see. The wisdom and advice we get from the females in our lives help us get a three-dimensional perspective on a situation, not just a male one-dimensional viewpoint. We must value and respect the opinions of the women around us. It is what these two men did, and it gave them the perspective they needed to successfully finish their mission.

4. WE NEED TO EXPRESS GRATITUDE AND APPRECIATION TO WOMEN.

The fourth thing we learn from these two men is to show gratitude and appreciation to the women in our lives just as the spies showed to Rahab for what she did.

> *So the men answered her, "Our lives for yours, if none of you tell this business of ours. And it shall be, when the LORD has given us the land, that we will deal kindly and truly with you."*

Rahab had risked her life and all she had to protect these two men. If caught, she would have faced certain death. These men realized they owed their lives to this brave woman, and they made sure she knew how grateful they were to her.

Showing gratitude to the women in our lives is extremely important. God has been showing me this is a major area I need to grow in. I grew up around a father who never showed any appreciation to anyone for anything, especially women. Instead of being appreciative and grateful to my mom for everything she did to run our house and family, he would constantly criticize her and put her down for everything she did. He would even make her lists of additional things he wanted done on top of all she had to do. He would call her from work and make sure she did them. He was abusive and cruel, never showing her any gratitude.

I grew up around this, and I have come to realize I didn't praise the women in my life enough. I expected them to praise me for all the things I did, but I didn't give them praise. I'm trying to improve in this area by being more thankful and complimentary toward them and for what they do. It's what a godly man needs to do.

When was the last time you showed your gratitude to the women in your life? This isn't just limited to a spouse. It applies to daughters, sisters, moms, friends, co-workers, any and all women. This lack of gratitude and appreciation by men is a gross sin against God and the women he has blessed us with.

We, as men, can no longer take for granted the women in our lives. We can't expect them to do what they do as if they are servants or lesser beings. We must appreciate them. We must praise them. We must let them know how grateful we are to them. We must even pitch in and help them and make their lives easier. To fail to do this is sin. It is also degrading and disrespectful to women. We must all work on this area. I know I certainly do.

So far we've learned that we need to show trust in women, show them dignity and respect, value their opinions, and show gratitude to them. This brings us to the fifth attitude.

5. WE NEED TO SEE WOMEN AS SPIRITUAL, NOT SEXUAL, BEINGS.

The final area to examine is one of the most important if we are to win the battle over sexual temptation. Look carefully at these verses.

> *Now Joshua the son of Nun sent out two men from Acacia Grove to spy secretly, saying, "Go, view the land, especially Jericho." So they went, and came to the house of a prostitute named Rahab, and lodged there.*

> *"...And as soon as we heard these things, our hearts melted; neither did there remain any more courage in anyone because of you, for the LORD your God, He is God in heaven above and on earth beneath. Now therefore, I beg you, swear to me by the LORD, since I have shown you kindness, that you also will show kindness to my father's house, and give me a true token, and spare my father, my mother, my brothers, my sisters, and all that they have, and deliver our lives from death."*

> *So the men answered her, "Our lives for yours, if none of you tell this business of ours. And it shall be, when the LORD has given us the land, that we will deal kindly and truly with you."*

These men didn't view Rahab as a sexual being, even though it clearly says she was a prostitute. Instead, they saw her as a person with a spiritual need. They promised to protect her and make her a part of Israel. They sought to fill her spiritual needs by making her one of God's children.

In the world in which we live, men are taught to always be seeking sex. That is as honest as I can put it. Real men snag the hot chick and have a one-night stand. A real man is a ladies' man, always looking for the next tryst with the hottest girl possible. Men of the world tend to look at women as sexual objects. They look at her body, her appeal, her sensuality, and they base their thoughts and opinions of her on these things. They don't think about her feelings or emotions. They ignore her needs and desires. They look at her as an object. This is sin. It is degrading. It is wrong and it must stop!

A godly man will act like Jesus acts. He will see women like Jesus sees them. These two spies never made any mention of Rahab's occupation. They didn't view her as a sexual conquest like a Hollywood movie spy would have. They see her as a spiritual being. They listened to her heart and heard her desire to follow their God. They ensured her safety and security so she could become a convert of the one true God.

We are all guilty of heinous sin when we view women as sexual objects. We must change our thought patterns and mindsets as we put on manhood.

Take a moment and think about it. If a man is watching a TV show, movie, or porn video, are his thoughts about how the women in the video would make him feel, or about how she feels?

Does he wonder why she places such a low value on herself by doing what she does?

Does he wonder what happened in her life to make her feel so worthless that all she thinks she is good for is arousing men?

Does it break his heart how hopeless and helpless she feels inside?

Does he ever think about how deceived and in bondage she is to sin?

Does he think that if she died while making this video she would spend eternity in hell?

Does he think about how he would feel if she were his sister or daughter?

Men need to wake up and think about these things. It should break our hearts to view women through these eyes. We should never see a scantily dressed woman in an enjoyable way. We also shouldn't look at her through self-righteous eyes and see her as a dirty or sinful thing to be despised or shunned. We should see her as a spiritual being with thoughts, emotions, feelings, dreams, and desires. We should not think provocative thoughts. Instead, our first thought should be to immediately ask God to save her and help her reach her full potential as a godly woman.

Do you find this teaching to be too extreme or hard? Then examine Jesus. He was a man just like us, tempted in every way. He had sexual urges and desires. However, he didn't exploit women in order to fulfill his needs.

When the prostitute bent over to wash his feet, I am sure he didn't sneak a peek at her cleavage. When left alone with an alleged adulterous woman, he didn't make any advances. When alone at a well with a promiscuous Samaritan woman, he never tried to take advantage of her. Instead, he immediately recognized the oppression she faced from men and sought to help her break free. He always addressed a woman's spiritual needs and sought to help her fulfill them.

He was a real man. He is the man we must follow. How do we do this? We do it by following Paul's advice in Romans 12:1–2:

I beseech you therefore, brethren, by the mercies of God, that you present your bodies a living sacrifice, holy, acceptable to God, which is your reasonable service. And do not be conformed to this world, but be transformed by the renewing of your mind, that you may prove what is that good and acceptable and perfect will of God (NJKV).

These verses are clear about what we need to do. To think about women in sexual terms, in the same way the world does, is conforming to the world. Unfortunately, many Christian men think about sex and women in a worldly way because of the constant exposure we discussed earlier. This is not what God wants. His good, acceptable, and perfect will is for us to renew our minds. We must retrain or reprogram our brains. How do we do this?

The number one way to do this is to aggressively read the Word of God. We need to get the truths found in the Bible into our heads. This is the only way to counter the constant barrage of worldly thinking we encounter every day.

Psalms 119:9 tells us the best way to clean up our mind is to read God's Word.

Psalms 119:140 tells us God's Word helps make us pure. We need to saturate our minds with the pure and holy Word of God. It points out wrong thought patterns and teaches us the right way to think.

The second way to go about renewing our minds is through prayer. We need to spend time daily talking to God. It's hard in the busy world in which we live to find the time for prayer, but we must do it. Prayer is the artery that connects our hearts to God. We need time in prayer so the Holy Spirit can show us areas that need to be renewed. Prayer also helps us in times of temptation. It is the best weapon we have. We can cry out to our Advocate for help. Praying is vital; we need to do it.

The final action that helps us renew our mind is to eliminate the worldliness from our lives. We, as Christian men, are tolerating too much worldliness. We can renew our mind by cutting out a lot of the TV and

We as men can no longer take for granted the women in our lives. We must let them know how grateful we are to them. We must even pitch in and help them and make their lives easier. To fail to do this is sin.

movies we watch. As a matter of fact, I want to give you this challenge. For one month, don't watch any television or see any movies. Instead, spend the time reading the Bible and praying. This is a tough challenge, but you will be stunned at the end of the month how much stronger your conscience will be and how much less you will be able to watch. I urge you to give it a shot.

> **We are all guilty of heinous sin when we view women as sexual objects. We must change our thought patterns and mindsets so we put on manhood.**

As we come to a close, I want you to examine yourself. Did this chapter strike a chord in your spirit? Are there areas you need to face, change, and conquer? This is the convicting power of the Holy Spirit...*do not ignore it!* Face the areas he is exposing and make drastic changes. Deal dramatically with the areas he addresses.

What do I mean by *deal with it dramatically*? Well, Mark 9:43 says if your right hand offends you, cut it off. This is not a command for self-mutilation. It means getting rid of whatever causes you to sin, even if it hurts.

If pornography on the Internet causes you to sin, get rid of the Internet. While the Internet is handy, people got along for centuries without it, and if it causes you to sin, better to lose Google temporarily than to lose your soul eternally.

If movies are causing you to look at women in a childish, degrading way, cut them off at the knees. No one ever died from not watching a movie that degrades women. But many souls have been trapped and died because they filled their minds with unholiness and an ungodly portrayal of women and how they deserved to be treated. We have to do whatever it takes to eliminate the things that feed degradation of women in our lives!

We must learn new ways of thinking about the opposite sex. We must learn to put our trust in the women around us. We must always treat them with dignity and respect. We must value their thoughts and opinions. We must express gratitude and appreciation for both who they are and what they do. Finally, we must look at women as spiritual, not sexual beings. When we make these changes to our thinking and behavior, we will have gone a long way to putting aside our childish ways and putting on manhood. There is no better time to start than today!

GROUP STUDY QUESTIONS

1. Is sexual sin a sin of the mind, a sin of the eyes, or both? Explain your answer.

2. Do you struggle with trusting women or allowing yourself to rely on women?

3. Point two stated, "we need to treat women with dignity, not disgrace." What does this mean to you?

4. Do you ever struggle to let women give you wisdom and guidance? Do you think you know more than them? What is usually the result of this mindset?

5. How often do you express gratitude to the women in your life?

6. This chapter discussed treating women as spiritual, not sexual beings and listed questions of what a man's thoughts are when he sees something sexual. What jumped out or convicted you the most in that list?

7. Which of the five points discussed in this chapter do you struggle with the most?

8. What can we as a group do to help you in this area?

9. Will we as a group commit to take the one-month challenge to give up all TV and movies and replace this time with prayer and Bible reading?

·10·

IT COSTS A LOT TO BE FREE

Have you ever thought something you believed was true, but then later found out it actually was not a fact? For example, I was recently doing some research on the Revolutionary War and the Fourth of July and found a few such "facts." Here are some of the interesting items on the list:

1. George Washington didn't have wooden teeth.

As a fact...he had four different sets of dentures: gold, hippopotamus ivory, lead, and both human and animal teeth.

2. The Declaration of Independence was not signed on July 4, 1776.

As a fact...Americans formally declared independence from Britain on July 2, 1776, upon the passage of the Lee Resolution. Although the Declaration of Independence is dated July 4, that's simply the day the Continental Congress adopted the document's language (basically, the final draft). Thanks to James Madison's journals, most historians believe that signing did not begin until August 2, 1776.

117

3. Paul Revere didn't ride around shouting, "The British are coming!"

As a fact...Paul rode mostly in silence to avoid army patrols while spreading the word. When speaking to people along his route to Concord, he used the much less catchy, "The regulars are coming out" as a warning.

4. The Liberty Bell did not crack on July 4, 1776.

As a fact...the bell cracked shortly after it was delivered due to being improperly cast when made.

Interesting, isn't it? There were quite a few things on the list that I believed were true because I heard them stated so many times. I was surprised to see I had been convinced of something that wasn't actually a fact.

Unfortunately, this can also happen in our spiritual lives. We hear something stated over and over by other believers that we come to believe is true, but if we examine it against what the Bible really says, it is totally different. In this chapter, we are going to see one of the misconceptions keeping God's men in their childish ways and from putting on manhood. Once we debunk this false belief, we will be better equipped to live a life worthy of the calling.

What is this belief? The belief is that our freedom in Christ gives us freedom to do anything we want because we are no longer under the law.

In Romans 8:1, Paul states, *There is now no condemnation for those who are in Christ Jesus.* In the verses preceding this, he discusses how his sinful desires cause him to do things he doesn't want to do. As a result, many people, especially those who grew up in a very legalistic, religious background, use these verses as the basis for a teaching that says their freedom in Christ allows them to do what they want, watch what they want, and act however they want because there is no condemnation for a believer.

These believers don't want to be told certain actions or behaviors are sinful and a believer needs to stop them. When confronted, they flip to the back of Romans and show you where Paul discusses weaker brothers and stronger brothers. Like a picky eater at a smorgasbord buffet, they pick what they like and leave the rest behind. As a result, we are growing a generation of weak, worldly Christians who see holiness as a dirty word as they stay stuck in their childish ways. This is not God's will for his sons.

Like it or not, God requires a change in actions and behavior in his children. He has rules, regulations, and standards he wants us to live by in our daily walk. I am not talking about being legalistic. Trust me, as someone who attended a Christian school with legalistic beliefs such as women should never cut their hair, and men always need to wear long-sleeve shirts, I understand the legalism people try to avoid. However, we can't swing the pendulum so far the other way that we go from being legalistic to being "anything-goes" Christians. Such a man is not living a life worthy of the calling.

Paul himself understood this. When asked if our freedom in Christ gives us room to live more liberally, he emphatically declared "God forbid!"

Paul understood freedom in Christ doesn't give us freedom to mess with sin; it gives us freedom to leave sin and pursue a life of godliness. We are free to follow and serve God on the narrow road Jesus describes in the Gospels. It allows us to walk away from sin and follow Jesus. It gives us freedom to be Jesus's servant.

You see, freedom in Christ is freedom from sin's control. Christian freedom is freedom *from* sin, not freedom *to* sin. As Martin Luther put it, "Freedom is not the right to do what you want, but rather the power to do what you ought."

Sin can no longer have control of our lives. We have the ability to resist temptation, leave our lives of sin, our bondages, our iniquities, the things that ruin our lives on a daily basis. These things no longer own us and control us because Christ set us free. So why would we use this freedom to stay bound? This is the exact question Paul answers in the book of Galatians.

Galatians 5:13 says, *You, my brothers and sisters, were called to be free. But do not use your freedom to indulge the flesh.*

Romans 6:1–2 says, *What shall we say, then? Shall we go on sinning so that grace may increase? By no means! We are those who have died to sin; how can we live in it any longer?*

Paul never taught that we have freedom to continue sinning. He never gave believers license to do whatever they want because they have freedom in Christ. On the contrary! Paul constantly and consistently taught that a believer's obligation was to leave his or her former way of life behind and begin a new legacy of godliness. Paul would be appalled at those who say it is okay to sin because of freedom in Christ! He knew the cost of Christianity! He didn't take numerous floggings, stoning, imprisonment, and persecution to have the right to sin.

"But Jamie, Paul says in Romans 14 he is convinced nothing is unclean and believers shouldn't stop other believers from doing something that doesn't hurt their conscience." Well, let's look at the passage:

Accept the one whose faith is weak, without quarreling over disputable matters. One person's faith allows them to eat anything, but another, whose faith is weak, eats only vegetables. The one who eats everything must not treat with contempt the one who does not, and the one who does not eat everything must not judge the one who does, for God has accepted them (Romans 14:1–3).

The key phrase for this passage is "disputable matters." Paul is not giving a license for stronger Christians to sin. He is referring to things not clearly defined in the Bible.

In Paul's day, these issues were dietary laws and Jewish holidays. Today, some disputable issues could be things like modern worship. Some feel it is wrong to sing anything but hymns, others do not. This is a disputable matter. Another issue might be church apparel. Some feel you have to wear a suit and tie to church; others feel jeans are okay...this is a disputable matter and shouldn't rip a church apart.

When I was in high school, I went to a Christian school that was a "holiness school." They had some very strict beliefs, like guys had to wear long-sleeve shirts and women had to wear dresses and have long hair, etc. My family didn't have these beliefs. However, the people at the school did. One woman I knew was extremely strict about it. She felt in order to serve God wholeheartedly, she had to live this way. This was a belief she had, and to be honest, I respect how strongly she felt about it. So it would be sin for me to demand she cut her hair and wear pants, because it would kill her conscience.

Here's another example of a disputable issue. A few years ago I was waiting for the Super Bowl to start. I watched the news, and they had a story about how many prostitutes were hauled into the city hosting the Super Bowl, and how many young girls would be forced to prostitute themselves for men throughout the week of the Super Bowl at a staggeringly higher rate than usual. This story disgusted me and I decided I could not be part of it by watching the Super Bowl. It was my conviction, I didn't demand other Christians do it, but I also didn't let other Christians tell me I had to watch it.

Paul understood that freedom in Christ doesn't give us freedom to mess with sin; it gives us freedom to leave sin and pursue a life of godliness.

We have to be sure we don't use this verse as a license to sin. A disputable matter would be, "I can't watch the Super Bowl because women and young girls are trafficked into the city at a higher rate for further sexual entertainment." A non-disputable matter would be, "Can I engage in activity with a prostitute while I am at the sporting event?" See the difference?

Many believers think a lot of stuff is disputable that really isn't disputable. Some say "I can go watch this R-rated movie because it doesn't say in the Bible I can't." But this isn't true. The Bible says to avoid sexual immorality, extreme violence, to guard our mind, to not sit in the council of the ungodly. While it doesn't say "don't go to R-rated movies," it has a lot of principles that say the content in the movie is sin.

Freedom in Christ does not give us a license to sin. It doesn't remove the need for boundaries, morals, and convictions. When we excuse our sin under the heading of freedom of Christ, we are falling into a huge trap and lie of Satan, and it is keeping us stuck in our childish ways.

> **Paul would be appalled at those who say it is okay to sin because of freedom in Christ! He knew the cost of Christianity! He didn't take numerous floggings, stoning, imprisonment, and persecution to have the right to sin!**

So what does God require of us? God requires one thing of his sons. This one thing is what shows we are living a life worthy of the calling. What is it? **Obedience.**

God wants his sons to obey him. He wants us to obey the commands of the Bible. He wants us to live for him and show our gratitude to him for saving us by walking in obedience to his instructions found in his Word.

John 14:15 says, *If you love Me, keep My commandments* (NKJV).

1 John 3:24 states, *The one who keeps God's commands lives in him, and he in them.*

John 15:10 says, *If you keep My commandments, you will abide in My love, just as I have kept My Father's commandments and abide in His love* (NKJV).

God wants his children to obey him. He loves us and wants the best for us so much that he gave us the Bible to be our blueprint for life. The Bible is full of promises and encouragement, hope, comfort, and guidance, but it is also full of commandments. I'm not just talking about the Old Testament law; I am also talking about the New Testament. The New

Testament is full of passages that clearly say, "Do not do this, do not do that!"

For example, the end of Ephesians 4 and beginning of Ephesians 5 says:

> *Therefore each of you must put off falsehood and speak truthfully to your neighbor, for we are all members of one body. "In your anger do not sin": Do not let the sun go down while you are still angry, and do not give the devil a foothold. Anyone who has been stealing must steal no longer, but must work, doing something useful with their own hands, that they may have something to share with those in need.*
>
> *Do not let any unwholesome talk come out of your mouths, but only what is helpful for building others up according to their needs, that it may benefit those who listen. And do not grieve the Holy Spirit of God, with whom you were sealed for the day of redemption. Get rid of all bitterness, rage and anger, brawling and slander, along with every form of malice.*
>
> *Be kind and compassionate to one another, forgiving each other, just as in Christ God forgave you. Follow God's example, therefore, as dearly loved children and walk in the way of love, just as Christ loved us and gave himself up for us as a fragrant offering and sacrifice to God.*
>
> *But among you there must not be even a hint of sexual immorality, or of any kind of impurity, or of greed, because these are improper for God's holy people. Nor should there be obscenity, foolish talk or coarse joking, which are out of place, but rather thanksgiving. For of this you can be sure: No immoral, impure or greedy person—such a person is an idolater—has any inheritance in the kingdom of Christ and of God. Let no one deceive you with empty words, for because of such things God's wrath comes on those who are disobedient. Therefore do not be partners with them.*

That sure seems like a list of things we need to avoid doing in our lives. Freedom in Christ doesn't excuse us from obeying this list. What it does is give us the freedom from sin's clutches so we can obey God and his commandments.

God longs for his sons to begin walking in obedience. He wants us to stop swinging back and forth on the pendulum between legalism and liberalism and just do what the Bible says. He wants us to do it for one reason alone—because we love him.

In fact, this is love for God: to keep his commands. And his commands are not burdensome, for everyone born of God overcomes the world (1 John 5:3–4).

The positive side of this verse is that we show our love for God when we obey his commandments found in the Bible and stop following the ways of the world. The negative side is that if we don't obey God's commands then we do not truly love him. Our level of obedience is directly tied to our level of love for God. You can't say you love God if you are still living like the world!

Think I am being too extreme? Then let's look at Jesus's words. In John 15:14 Jesus said to his followers, *You are my friends if you do what I command.*

He asked the question in Luke 6:46, *Why do you call me "Lord, Lord," and do not do what I say?*

The missing ingredient in many men's spiritual walks is something called *sanctification.* Sanctification is a big theological word that essentially means every day we are to allow the Holy Spirit to point out areas of sin for us to face and deal with so we can change and become more like Jesus.

That is the believer's goal in life, to daily become more Christlike. We can't experience proper sanctification if we excuse every sin we commit. We have to read the Word, allow the Holy Spirit to convict us, and then walk in obedience and act differently. This is how we put on godly manhood. It enables us to live a life worthy of the calling.

This has been a really heavy chapter full of theology and doctrine, but it all boils down to one simple truth. God expects obedience from his sons. The question I have for you as we bring this chapter to a close is this: Will you overcome your childish ways?

Will you stop believing the misconception that freedom in Christ means you can live however you want?

Will you start showing your love for God by obeying his commandments?

Are you willing to spend the time necessary in the Word to learn how God wants you to live so you can walk in obedience?

Will you allow the Holy Spirit to convict you so you can be sanctified and made into the image of Jesus?

Will you live a life worthy of the calling and live in obedience to God? It is time God's men got off the legalism/liberalism pendulum and simply obey the Word of God. The question is, will you do it?

GROUP STUDY QUESTIONS

1. What do think the phrase "freedom in Christ" means?

2. Do believers have the freedom to do whatever they want whenever they want?

3. This chapter gave some examples of disputable matters. What are some areas you think are disputable matters? What are areas that are not disputable?

4. How does obedience coexist with our freedom in Christ?

5. We discussed sanctification and daily becoming more Christ-like. How do you see this happening in your life?

6. How can we as a group help you walk in obedience?

·11·

ENTITLED TO SERVE

A real man of God does what needs to be done, especially when he is the last person in the world who should have to do it. Why? Because he has a servant's heart.

This is something the Holy Spirit spoke to me a while back when I first started thinking about this book. It is so true. God's men are called to be servants. Only a man stuck in his childish ways thinks he deserves to be served and taken care of throughout life. A man who is living a life worthy of the calling understands that to put on manhood, he has to be a servant.

The simple truth of the matter is this: God never called anyone to be a master. He only calls people to serve. Our job as men of God is to be a servant. In this chapter, we'll look at why we need to serve and who we need to serve.

Let's start with the why. Why does a man who is putting on manhood need to serve others? The answer is quite simple. We are supposed to be following Jesus's example, and Jesus's life was the model of a man who served.

Jesus left the glory of heaven and came to earth to serve others. His entire life was geared to servanthood. It was the one lesson he constantly hammered into his disciples. Whenever they would go off on another I-am-the-most-important-disciple kick, he would gently remind them they were not called to be masters lording over others. Instead, they were called to serve the least among them.

The disciples struggled with this teaching because they thought, as Jesus's right-hand men, they deserved to have the least of these serving them. This childish attitude came from a lifetime of the Jewish elite pushing them down and lording over them. Now they were the bigwigs, Jesus's chosen men, and they were all up for being the top dog others served. However, Jesus never let them get away with it. Instead, he taught them what it means to serve and how to develop a servant's heart. He even demonstrated servanthood when he washed their feet.

If we are to model Jesus and put on manhood, we need to put aside our pride and humbly serve others. This is a man God can use, and this is the man who will influence other men around him and lead them to Christ. I remember a specific time when this was demonstrated right before my eyes.

It was during my junior year of college. During this time, the college was going through a lot of changes, one of which was the promotion of one of my favorite professors to the position of dean of men. This professor had only been at the school for three years, and already he was promoted to this huge position. However, he never allowed this to fill him with pride. He never lost his servant's heart and humble attitude.

It was the end of the semester. For the entire year, the guys on my floor had to endure a young, cocky freshman who constantly harassed the other guys on the floor. He would do stupid jokes and pranks like placing Vaseline on our doorknobs or waking us up in the middle of the night with prank phone calls. Eventually, we had had enough and some of the guys decided to take revenge.

Since it was the end of the semester, we had to get our rooms into the same shape we found them. Because our rooms were so small, many of the guys had placed their beds on cinder blocks, raising the bed higher off the ground. This provided much-needed storage space underneath the bed.

Now that the semester was almost over, they had to get rid of the blocks. Not wanting to waste the blocks, the guys took all of them and piled them in front of the young prankster's door, making a nice concrete wall. Then they "mortared" them together by filling the holes with popcorn. As a final touch, they smeared the freshman's favorite prank fluid, Vaseline, over the entire wall. It was a slimy, sticky mess.

When the freshman came back to the dorm and saw the wall, he was furious, which made the pranksters even more proud. This is where the new dean of men came into the picture. When he found out what had happened, he "suggested" that the guys remove the wall.

The guys refused. They were too proud to touch the slimy mess. They were upperclassmen who had pranked a lowly freshman for not showing them proper respect. However, their pride soon turned to shame.

God never called anyone to be a master. He only calls people to serve.

The newly appointed dean of men came into our dorm, removed his tie and jacket, rolled up his sleeves, and began taking apart the disgusting wall, becoming covered in Vaseline and popcorn in the process. As he carried the slimy blocks outside, all of the guys on the floor were filled with shame. Immediately, he had ten or more guys, myself included, carrying the mess to the Dumpster.

My professor-turned-dean-of-men didn't take pride in his new position. Instead, he had a humble attitude and a servant's heart. Unlike the proud students, he didn't think of himself as too good to do this disgusting job. Instead, he demonstrated humility and servanthood. No job was below him. We all need to learn from his example.

This professor is not the only example of a man with a servant's heart. A few years later, I came across another man who showed me what it means to serve.

I have a good friend who was also the leader of the men's ministry department in his state's denominational district. He had a position of authority and power in his district, and he had men looking up to him and hanging on his every word. Having gone to his district convention and speaking with the men under his influence, I can say that they would do anything for him because they admire him so much.

I remember the first time I went to this leader's convention. It was his first year as district leader. I arrived on Friday, the night he was scheduled to speak. Where do you think I found him when I arrived?

You would think he would be in the conference hall, eating up the praise and admiration of the men. Or maybe he'd be off by himself, because, as the speaker, he was above the rest of the men and didn't need to interact with them. But that isn't where I found him.

You know where he was? He was outside, in the street, helping men unload their cars and carrying their bags inside to the convention center. That is a heart of service. In his position, he could have told any number of men to go out and do this job, but he did it himself, because he knows his job is to serve, not be served.

Just last week I saw an amazing example of a man who understood the need for God's men to serve. I was at a women's event run by my denomination's district women's department. I was volunteering to help out while my sister, Adessa, led a workshop at the event. I spent the day in a dark sound booth where I could see everyone but no one could see me.

During this time, I watched a very important pastor who is also a denominational leader, serving at the event. I will admit, when I first saw that he was there, my cynical side wondered if he was there in his capacity as a district leader to take a few bows. However, he wasn't. I watched in awe as this man rolled up his sleeves, and worked as a busboy setting and clearing plates during the meals. He served diligently for three or four hours, and when his work was done, he left quietly with no fanfare. Not to mention the fact that the event was held at a large church very near to his large church, the "competition" as the world would say.

That is what we are talking about here! This man could have easily waltzed in and let everyone know who he was and why they should feel blessed to have him there. But he didn't. Instead he served without recognition. In fact, I am sure few even knew who the guy clearing the tables was, but I knew from working with him on Mantour Conferences. I was so impressed. He now has a fan for life!

God aches for a generation of men to rise up and be a generation of servants. The world has seen quite enough of God's men who think they are too good to get their hands dirty and serve others. He wants men with the heart of Jesus who realize no job, no task, no responsibility, nothing is below them. God wants men who lay down their lives with a heart of service to him.

This is a lesson I have had to learn in my own life. You see, I am the only son in my family. My relatives had always treated sons like they were princes. I'm not exaggerating. They spoiled boys, treated them like royalty, and taught them to expect such treatment. Strange, I know. Still, I grew up in this environment, and as a result, I learned how to be a taker, not a giver.

I expected people to serve me. I demanded people take care of me, do for me, and treat me well. I demanded respect. I never looked to serve others, but expected them to serve me, especially women.

Then I reached the point we discussed earlier where I realized what a wreck I was and how far I was from being a godly man. As God began working on my heart and removing years of junk and sin from inside of me, he started showing me how sinful my attitude of demanding others to serve me was, and how I was demeaning other people. He began teaching me a man of God cannot lord over others, but needs to be a man who serves. Then he took me through servant school. What do I mean?

Well, I learned to serve. I learned how to put other people's needs and desires above my own. You see, as I mentioned previously, my mom developed a severe environmental allergy during this time that made her extremely sensitive to smells. If she got around certain smells such as perfume or paint, her lungs would shut down and she would need to be rushed to a doctor immediately. So during this time, life revolved around taking care of my mom and making sure she never got around anything with a smell.

While this was a horrible situation for my mom, God took this evil and used it for some good, because I had to learn how to have life not revolve around me and my desires, but rather revolve around serving others. My schedule, my activities, my way of life, everything had to change because my mom needed my sister and me to take care of her.

God used this time in my life to develop a servant's heart. He transformed an arrogant, selfish kid and made me into a man who serves people on a daily basis. I know if he did this for me, he will do it for you, too!

So now that we have learned why we need to be servants, let's switch gears and see who we are to serve.

1. WE ARE TO SERVE GOD

You are probably thinking, "Duh!" We all know we need to serve God. But do we really know what this means?

You see, serving God is more than just going to church and reading the Bible. I am in no way diminishing those two areas. They are *huge!* They need to be a part of every man's life. But we serve God in more ways than this. One of the biggest ways we serve God is to stop treating his heart's desire for us as the Great Option instead of what it really is, the Great Commission!

Matthew 28:18 says, *Then Jesus came to them and said, "All authority in heaven and on earth has been given to me. Therefore go and make disciples of all nations, baptizing them in the name of the Father and of the Son and of the Holy Spirit, and teaching them to obey everything I have commanded you."*

This passage is a commission to serve. We are to serve God by reaching the lost world and sharing with them the gospel that can change their entire lives. This job is not just for preachers and pastors. It is everyone's job! We serve God by serving the lost world and pointing them toward a Savior. We need to make ourselves available to the lost and serve them to help them become believers.

How do we serve the lost? There are countless ways. You could volunteer to work in a soup kitchen or homeless shelter. Maybe you could volunteer to drive people to church. You could invite a friend to a church activity, and pay his way. The possibilities are endless for ways you can serve God by reaching out to the lost around you. Ask God to show you ways you can serve him by helping others. I guarantee he will answer this prayer, because it lines up with his will.

2. WE ARE TO SERVE OUR FAMILIES

This concept was a foreign notion to me twenty years ago. I never served any of my family members. Instead, I expected and demanded they serve me. Unfortunately, many men have the same attitude.

Men of God, we cannot continue expecting the precious ones God has blessed us with to serve us. We are to serve them.

Ephesians 5 has some great teaching on how a man needs to treat his family. Let's look at the different relationships.

Husbands, love your wives, just as Christ loved the church and gave himself up for her to make her holy, cleansing her by the washing with water through the word, and to present her to himself as a radiant church, without stain or wrinkle or any other blemish, but holy and blameless. In this same way, husbands ought to love their wives as their own bodies. He who loves his wife loves himself.

133

This is an excellent passage to show how a man serves his wife. Paul says a husband needs to love his wife like Jesus loved the church. To get the full meaning of this passage, we need to understand how Jesus loved the church.

When Jesus was on earth, his entire life revolved around serving. If we study the Gospels, we can see ways he served the church that we can apply to our relationships.

First, he put their needs above his needs. Jesus constantly had thousands of people coming to him and needing his help and assistance. They had urgent needs and they needed his miraculous power to help them. Jesus never turned them away. Even when he was tired or hungry, he put their needs and issues above his needs.

Here is an interesting way to serve your wife that few men ever think about as being service. How many of you have ever had your wife come to you and dump all of her emotions and feelings out on you and tell you exactly what she thinks of you and what you are doing? I know you all have had this happen; I am single and I have had this happen!

Often our response is to lash back in kind. However, next time we need to follow Jesus's example and not respond in kind. We serve our wives, sisters, mothers, and daughters by instead listening and then trying to help.

When did Jesus do this? We see a perfect example in the John 11.

Jesus and his men are on the road doing their thing when a messenger runs up to Jesus with some news. His good friend Lazarus is gravely ill and his sisters, Mary and Martha, want Jesus there to heal him ASAP!

Instead of returning with the messenger right away, Jesus stays where he is for two days. By the time he makes it to Lazarus's house, Lazarus was dead. Needless to say, Mary and Martha were not too thrilled with Jesus.

"Lord," Martha said to Jesus, "if you had been here, my brother would not have died..."

When Mary reached the place where Jesus was and saw him, she fell at his feet and said, "Lord, if You had been here, my brother would not have died."

These two distraught women lash out at Jesus, blaming him for the death of their brother! Instead of lashing out in anger at them, Jesus saw through their tongue lashing to the pain behind it and instead ministered to their need. He served their need instead of reacting to their action. Guys, we need to do the same thing.

Jesus served the church in so many ways, and all of them can be applied to our relationships. God's men need to start serving their wives in the same way Jesus served the church.

Paul's words in Ephesians don't just stop at how we serve our wives. He has more to say.

Children, obey your parents in the Lord, for this is right. "Honor your father and mother"—which is the first commandment with a promise— "so that it may go well with you and that you may enjoy long life on the earth."

I know what you're thinking. "Wait a minute Jamie, this passage is about how my kids need to treat me!"

Well, my question in response is this: Were you hatched in an egg?

Even if you are married with kids, you are still the child of someone. So this verse applies to you too.

It's a child's responsibility to show respect to his parents and serve them when possible. Now, if you are like me and come from an abusive background, you're probably freaking out right now! I know years ago I would have been. But even if your parents were abusive, you still need to serve them in love.

I am not saying you need to allow them to abuse you, control you, or mistreat you. What I am saying is you need to treat them with dignity and respect. You have to honor your parents. You need to be there to help them when they need help, and to show them the love of God.

I had to come to the place where I would decide to do this in my life. Serving my mom was easy. She was a loving, devoted mom who was sick and needed help. However, serving my dad was another thing altogether.

After my mom died, I had to face this area of my life. To be honest with you, my attitude at that point was, "I am outta here!" My dad was on his own as far as I was concerned. He had been my abuser my whole life, he had abused my mom till the day she died, and when she went to heaven, I was done!

However, God had other plans. He told me point blank, "You are not going to abandon your dad. You are going to stay with him and show him my forgiveness and godly love!"

I had to obey God and show the love of God to my dad. I won't lie: it is hard, but God wants me honoring him and serving him, so I obey.

Now, **I do not allow my dad to abuse me**. That is a crucial point. But I do show him honor and respect as my father, even though I do not agree with or excuse his life choices. Why do I do it? Because God calls his men to serve.

A man of God needs to also serve his children. This goes in direct opposition to our culture, which teaches children should serve their parents, but parents needs to sacrificially make their children a priority second only in their relationship to Jesus and help them in any way possible.

A quick side note before we look at the third group we need to serve: when I say parents should serve their kids, I do not mean they need to spoil them. Serving does what is best for them. Spoiling is not what is best. All spoiling children does is teach them to be served, and when they grow up, they won't have a servant's heart. What a parent needs to do is set an example of service that the child will learn and carry on when they grow up.

3. WE ARE TO SERVE OUR CHURCH

The final area where men of God need to be serving is in their local churches. God wants his men to be more than just a butt in the pew. He wants us to serve other believers. He wants us investing our time in others to help them grow in their walk with God.

The good news: I have never heard of a church that refuses help. There are loads of ways to serve.

Maybe you are thinking, "I don't think I can serve in a church. I can't preach or teach." Maybe you can't do these things, but there are endless ways you can serve that don't even involve these activities. What do I mean?

Do weeds grow at your church? Of course they do! You could serve the church by pulling weeds.

Do you know how to fix cars? You could maintain your church's vehicles.

God wants us to serve other believers. He wants us investing our time into others to help them grow in their walk with God.

Are you handy with a paintbrush? I am sure your church has a room in need of some sprucing up. Are you a good handyman? Churches have loads of projects that need to be worked on.

Manual labor not your thing? What about working with your church's boys' ministry or youth ministry as an adult helper? You could influence the lives of so many young men who are longing for the attention and approval of a godly man.

You could volunteer to come to church fifteen minutes early and greet people. You could offer to be the person who pours the grape juice into the cups on Communion Sunday. The ways to serve your church are innumerable. All you have to be is willing to serve.

"But Jamie, my life is jam-packed as it is! How am I supposed to find time to do volunteer work?" This can be answered in one word…**sacrifice**. Spoiler alert: that's the topic of our final chapter. But for this chapter, all I will say is you will need to sacrifice in other areas of your life so you can put on manhood and serve others.

Serving others must be a priority in our lives. Why? Because Jesus made it a priority, and we are supposed to be working daily toward becoming more like Jesus. In order to do this, we have to be willing to serve others.

You can never truly put on manhood if you refuse to serve others. This chapter has laid out three areas we need to focus on in order to develop a servant's heart. We have identified a few practical ways to do it. The question is, will you become a man with a servant's heart? Are you willing to serve others? I have made my choice, and now you have to do the same.

GROUP STUDY QUESTIONS

1. How did Jesus model being a servant to us? What are some examples from the Bible?

2. How can you serve the unsaved to help them become believers?

3. What are some practical ways you can serve your wife?

4. How can you have a servant's heart toward your parents? What emotions does this question evoke inside of you?

5. How do you serve your children without spoiling them?

6. How can you serve your church? What skills do you have that you can use to serve?

7. How can we as a group help you develop a servant's heart?

·12·

THE HEART OF
PUTTING ON MANHOOD

We have almost reached the end of our journey together in this book, but our journey is in no way complete. You see, the act of putting on manhood is not a once-and-done event. It's a lifelong process. Every day you will need to choose to put on manhood. Why do I say this?

I say it because it is true. We all have a sinful nature which is bound and determined to keep us stuck in our childish ways. The enemy will use every trick imaginable to appeal to our sinful nature. He will use lies, deceit, temptations, pride, anything and everything he can to keep you from putting on manhood. Why? **Because there is nothing Satan fears more than men who are working on laying aside their sins and breaking free of their bondages!** He *hates* when a man realizes his potential in God and grows into a strong man of God who walks in spiritual maturity. He knows such a man can't be stopped!

Satan knows such a man will not only work to change his own life, but he will also do everything in his power to help other men break free and experience the same level of freedom he has received in Christ. Slowly, man by man, change happens, revival takes place, and the world will never be the same!

Satan gets what we often don't. We are an unstoppable army when we leave our childish ways behind us and become mature, strong men of God.

Satan gets this, and he is terrified of it becoming a reality, so he throws everything plus the kitchen sink at God's men as soon as they start to put on manhood. I would bet many of you have experienced increased trials, struggles, and temptations as soon as you started reading this book. This happened because Satan is trying to get you preoccupied so you can't grow into a mature man of God.

Satan *hates* when a man realizes his potential in God and grows into a strong man of God who walks in spiritual maturity. He knows such a man can't be stopped!

That is why we need to put on manhood *daily*. Each day, we need to get up, look in the mirror, and say, "I choose today to put on manhood. I am going to do whatever it takes to follow God. I am not going to be sidetracked by the world around me. My focus is on God and where he leads me!"

To be able to do this and mean it, we need to look at one more lesson a man of God must practice to live a life worthy of the calling as he puts on manhood. What is this lesson? We need to learn to be men who sacrifice.

When I think of sacrifice, my mind goes to the Old Testament accounts of the nation of Israel building an altar and killing an animal on the altar. That's not necessarily the kind of sacrifice we are talking about in this final chapter. Yet in some ways it is.

You see, men like Abraham and Elijah didn't build altars for sacrifices for the fun of it. Trust me, it was not a fun job. You had to gather big heavy rocks and pile them on top of each other. Then you had to find some wood to put on the altar to start the fire. Then you had to have an animal present, kill it, and offer it. It was hard, dirty, sweaty work. When it was over, you were covered in dirt, blood, sweat, and soot. Making a sacrifice was not an easy thing. It took work, preparation, sweat, and effort.

In today's day and age, we don't have to make physical sacrifices. We don't have to labor and sweat to build a structure. We don't have to slaughter an animal. However, for us to be men who put on manhood, we do have to kill something in order to make sacrifices. What do I mean?

A man of God needs to be a man who sacrifices himself for others. He has to be willing to sacrifice his wants, his desires, his time, and his wishes in order to serve others. This goes totally against our nature.

Sacrificing goes along with what we discussed in the last chapter: servanthood. Just like we have to go against our sinful nature which yearns to be served, we must sacrifice ourselves, our wishes, our desires, our appetites, in order to daily put on manhood.

Are you unsure of how to do it? Luckily for us, we have a big brother to show us how.

Jesus sacrificed everything for us. He sacrificed his majesty in heaven sitting at the right hand of the Father when he came down to earth in bodily form. Think about that! He was part of the Trinity, fully God, with all power and authority. He daily had angels bowing and worshiping him.

However, he knew the ache in his Father's heart because of the separation sin had caused between the Father and mankind. He knew the longing his Father had to be reunited with mankind. But he also knew someone had to pay the price for man's treasonous sins. So Jesus left the glory and majesty of heaven and came to earth to be born in a dirty barn and wear messy diapers. The Deity who had all power became powerless and dependent on a mother for life and support.

He sacrificed his right to rule and reign and became submissive to his parental authority. The God who helped create the world took correction and rebuke from his parents. The One who had heavenly beings serving him came to earth and worked for a living to support his family after his father died. The Deity who helped create the trees of the earth now manually worked the wood into chairs and tables in the carpenter's shop.

The One who had created reproduction now had to battle sexual urges and desires. The One who had lived in utter holiness lived under constant disgrace from his virgin birth. Jesus sacrificed so much for each of us.

He sacrificed every waking minute of the day serving others, reaching out to the lost, and in ministry. The One who knew utter holiness came to earth and ministered to the tormented, the oppressed, the people bound in the worst evil and horror anyone could imagine. He came face to face with the evil that had no place whatsoever in his heavenly home.

He sacrificed sleep, food, recreation, and rest in order to reach more people. Through it all, he allowed himself to be maligned, degraded, rebuked, and despised by the "religious people" who he knew had no clue about true religion.

He made the ultimate sacrifice, when he, a sinless, perfect Man, died on the cross in our place. He was sacrificed on the cross. He was beaten, bruised, cursed, ridiculed, and mutilated as a sacrifice for each of us. Jesus literally put on manhood when he became flesh and dwelt among us, and his entire life was geared to sacrifice and serving others. He wants us to do the same.

The thrust of the message of putting on manhood is just that: sacrifice. We sacrifice our time to develop a relationship with God. It is literally impossible to spend time in relationship with God if we don't sacrifice something else to do it. All time is spent on something, so in order to spend it with God, we sacrifice something else.

We sacrifice our own wants, needs, and desires to take care of our family. The heart of a family man is totally a heart of sacrifice. The family's wants, needs, and desires are the most important thing in our lives, and often we sacrifice our own needs and we do without to meet their needs. That is the heart of a man who is putting on manhood!

We sacrifice our time and interests when we show our devotion to God by working in his church. It takes time to plan activities or to participate in things at church, and we have to sacrifice other things to make this time.

We sacrifice our self-sufficiency when we learn to rely on other men and develop our band of brothers. Our pride goes on the altar when we allow ourselves to be vulnerable and open with the other men in our lives.

We sacrifice our will when we surrender ourselves to the power of the Holy Spirit, when we let him fill us with his power and move through us, and we sacrifice our old sinful ways and tendencies when we begin living a life worthy of the calling. However, the reward of our sacrifice is that we grow and mature and become the godly men God desires for us to be.

We need to understand what a sacrifice really is. A sacrifice involves giving up something valuable and important to you for somebody or something you consider to be of more value or importance.

- We sacrifice our TV time to spend quality time with our kids.
- We sacrifice our time perusing Facebook to have a meaningful conversation with our wives.
- We sacrifice our fantasy football to spend more time in the Word and in prayer.
- We sacrifice the chance to go to Wednesday evening service to instead work with the young boys who need a man to love them and show them what it means to be a godly man.
- We sacrifice our Starbucks in order to stay within the confines of our budget.

These are just a few suggestions of what it means to sacrifice. It is taking something we enjoy and appreciate and giving it up so we can instead focus on the job of putting on manhood.

Sacrifice is not natural to any man. Our sinful nature screams for us to make it all about ourselves and to stay in our childish ways. It doesn't come naturally to put God and others before ourselves. But it is how we put on manhood.

Years ago, a man went for marriage counseling because of some issues he was having with his wife. The counselor said something to him that I never forgot when he shared it with me. He said, "You say you would be willing to die for your wife if need be. The question I have for you is this: You say you would die for her, but are you willing to live for her?"

He was asking the man if he was willing to sacrifice for his wife and live every day of his life for her. Would he be a man of sacrifice? This question could be applied to every area of a man's life.

The Bible says it this way. *Greater love hath no man than this, that a man lay down his life for his friends* (John 15:13 KJV).

Greater love has no man than this: that a man lay down his life to spend time with God.

Greater love has no man than this: that a man lay down his life for his wife.

Greater love has no man than this: that a man lay down his life for his children.

Greater love has no man than this: that a man lay down his life for the fellow believers in his local church.

Greater love has no man than this: that a man lay down his life for the men in his band of brothers.

Greater love has no man than this: that a man lay down his life and allow the Holy Spirit to lead and guide him.

Greater love has no man than this: that a man lay down his life by walking in obedience to God's commands.

Greater love has no man than this: that a man lay down his life and spend his money wisely and is a good steward.

Greater love has no man than this: that a man lay down his emotions and anger, and forgives.

Why do I reword the verse this way? Because by doing these things you are laying your life down for friends, family, fellow believers, and most of all, God. You can't truly put on manhood without being a man who is willing to sacrifice.

A man who has a heart that is willing to sacrifice anything and everything is a man Satan fears. Why? Because he knows he is a man who means business. He understands that this kind of man holds nothing or no one above his relationship with God and his ability to serve others. He is scared to death of God's men learning the incredible power they have if they will be men who sacrifice anything and everything for the sake of God's kingdom.

This is life and death stuff! This is spiritual warfare on its greatest level. It is what God called us to do.

God is crying out for his men to rise up and say, "Enough is enough! I am tired of being bound and defeated by the same sins and traps. I am tired of Satan kicking my butt! I am going to rise up and put on manhood! I am going to change how I live my life. I am going to sacrifice anything and everything I need to sacrifice in order to become the man of God I am destined to be."

> **A man who has a heart that is willing to sacrifice anything and everything is a man Satan fears. Why? Because he knows he's a man who means business.**

God is waiting for such a man! He longs for us all to get to the place where we will stand up and scream with every ounce of strength in our body and every breath of air we breathe, "When I was a child, I talked like a child, I thought like a child, I reasoned like a child. But I am not a child anymore! **I am putting on manhood!**"

GROUP STUDY QUESTIONS

1. Why is sacrifice such a big part of putting on manhood?

2. What are some areas you could sacrifice to develop a deeper walk with God?

3. What can you sacrifice to spend more time with your family?

4. What is something you could never imagine sacrificing? What if God asked you to sacrifice this area?

5. How can we as a group help you develop a sacrificing heart?

6. Are you committed to daily putting on manhood?

PUTTING ON
MANHOOD

SMALL GROUP WORKBOOK

SMALL GROUP ▪ 1 ▪ WORKBOOK

When I was a child, I talked like a child, I thought like a child, I reasoned like a child. When I became a man, I put the ways of childhood behind me (1 Corinthians 13:11).

Therefore, since we are surrounded by such a great cloud of witnesses, let us throw off everything that hinders and the sin that so easily entangles. And let us run with perseverance the race marked out for us (Hebrews 12:1).

One of the biggest things entangling men today is _____

_____

When we fall prey to the stereotypes of what a "real man" is according to the world, we are not allowing the _____ _____ to make us into what *he wants* us to be. Instead, we are letting the _____define us.

Stereotype: Men don't read to learn and grow.

Truth: We need to _____ and _____ God's Word.

Stereotype: Men _____, their wives just have to get used to it. Men can't help it.

Truth: Men can control their _____ and what they _____ _____.

I made a covenant with my eyes not to look lustfully at a young woman (Job 31:1).

Stereotype: Men can't _____. Our natural tendency is to conquer women, so how can we be expected to be with only one woman at a time?

Truth: God created _____ in the Garden of Eden, and designed it to be a monogamous _____ commitment.

> *Give honor to marriage, and remain faithful to one another in marriage. God will surely judge people who are immoral and those who commit adultery* (Hebrews 13:4 NLT).

> *Sex is as much spiritual mystery as physical fact. As written in Scripture, "The two become one." Since we want to become spiritually one with the Master, we must not pursue the kind of sex that avoids commitment and intimacy, leaving us lonelier than ever—the kind of sex that can never "become one"* (1 Corinthians 6:16 The Message).

Stereotype: Men don't have time to _____ or _____. Our society is too fast paced and we have too much to do.

Truth: We find _____ for things that are a _____.

But seek first his [God's] kingdom and his righteousness, and all these things will be given to you as well (Matthew 6:33).

Stereotype: Men aren't_____. We don't_____ or get emotionally involved.

Truth: Real men have _____ —that's the way God _____ us.

*When Jesus saw her weeping, and the Jews who had come along with
her also weeping, he was deeply moved in spirit and troubled.*
    "Where have you laid him?" he asked.
    "Come and see, Lord," they replied.
    Jesus wept (John 11:33–35).

*And when He came near the gate of the city, behold, a dead man was
being carried out, the only son of his mother; and she was a widow. And
a large crowd from the city was with her. When the Lord saw her, He
had compassion on her...* (Luke 7:12–13 NKJV).

God is calling men from around the world to become a new

_____ to this generation, men who are leav-

ing their old life behind, men who are abandoning the ways of the world

and pursuing the ways of God.

▪———— GROUP STUDY QUESTIONS ————▪

1. What are some of the things that entangle you and keep you from
   growing in your walk with God?

2. What steps can you take to break free from these entanglements?

3. How can we as a group help you?

4. We listed some of the stereotypes men face. What are some additional stereotypes?

5. What stereotype affects you the most?

6. Are you committed to the journey of putting on manhood?

SMALL GROUP ▪2▪ WORKBOOK

The first question we need to ask ourselves when we decide to put on manhood is how _____ are we _____ to go?

Joshua 24:15–23

Joshua gives them three choices:

Choice #1: Serve the gods of their _____. These gods are _____ _____ iniquities we observed growing up.

Choice #2: Serve the gods of the _____.

Choice #3: Serve the _____. This was the choice Joshua made, but every person had to choose for themselves.

It is easy to make a decision in the heat of the moment, but we have to count the_____. Can we keep the _____ we make?

We need to make the decision in our lives to put aside our childish things and pursue God _____. We can't let any-thing keep us from developing a heart that places no _____ on how far we will go with God.

We all need to ask ourselves, how far will we go for God? Will we go part way, or will we be totally _____ and _____ to him?

GROUP STUDY QUESTIONS

1. What are some things that have kept you from following God wholeheartedly?

2. What can you do to eliminate these barriers?

3. What are some of the cultural gods keeping you from wholeheartedly following God?

4. What are generational issues that keep you from following God without reservation?

5. This chapter listed some areas God may ask you to submit to him…what are some other areas God may ask of you to get you to serve him with all your heart?

6. What can the group do to help you wholeheartedly serve God?

SMALL GROUP ▪3▪ WORKBOOK

Priorities: If you don't put the big rocks in_____, you'll never get them in at all.

In the lives of godly men, what should the big rocks be?

Our number one priority in life, the one thing that takes precedence over anything else, even family, needs to be _____

_____

When we say we don't have time for reading the _____, what we are really saying is the cares of the world are more important to us than _____.

The second big rock, or the next priority we as men need to focus on, is our _____.

The third priority, or big rock, is our _____

_____.

Our job is not where we get our identity. We get that first from God, then from our families. Our job is where we get _____ to _____.

The fourth big rock, or fourth priority, is _____/

_____.

Matthew 28:18–20 says *Then Jesus came to them and said, "All authority in heaven and on earth has been given to me. Therefore go and make disciples of all nations, baptizing them in the name of the Father and of the Son and of the Holy Spirit, and teaching them to obey everything I have commanded you."*

_____, mentoring, and discipleship need to become a big rock in our lives.

These four priorities have to take precedence in your life, then the other things, the trivial things, the gravel, sand, and water, can fill up the rest.

GROUP STUDY QUESTIONS

1. What are the big rocks in your life right now?

2. Is spending time with God a big rock in your life? If not, what steps can you take to make this a priority?

3. What can you sacrifice to make time spent with God a priority? How can we as a group help you keep this commitment?

4. This chapter made the statement, "Your wife should be able to rely on you for spiritual guidance, and your kids should see in you how to have a walk with God." Is this statement true of your life? What would your wife and kids say if they were asked this question?

5. Do you use your career to meet needs inside of you?

6. Is mentorship/discipleship a big rock in your life?

7. Who is discipling you, and who are you discipling?

8. What can we as a group do to help you get your priorities straight and keep them straight?

SMALL GROUP ·4· WORKBOOK

"Show me who you spend your _____ with and I will show you who you are."

I Corinthians 15:33 says, *Do not be misled: "Bad company corrupts good character."* The obvious counterpoint to this is that _____ _____ company will encourage good _____ _____.

In order to put on manhood, we have to be devoted to the things of _____.

A man of God is committed to his local _____. We all need to be part of a _____ - _____ _____.

God is looking for men who go from sitting in a _____, taking from others, to men who are willing to give to other believers in the church and help them.

We live in childish ways when we _____ a body of believers, but we are putting on manhood when we _____ _____ ourselves to God.

GROUP STUDY QUESTIONS

1. The chapter discussed the quote, "Show me who you spend your time with, and I will show you who you are." How does this quote apply to your life before you got saved?

2. How does this quote apply to your life now?

3. What is the difference between following God wholeheartedly and being devoted to God?

4. How devoted to God are you?

5. What are some ways you can become more active in your church?

6. What are some unique gifts and abilities you have, and how could they benefit the church you attend?

7. What can we as a group do to help you grow in your devotion to God?

SMALL GROUP ▪5▪ WORKBOOK

A real man who is focused on putting on manhood understands he needs

other _____ who _____ alongside

him as they travel together toward becoming godly men.

No man is an _____! We can't _____

_____ our way through life. Even the Lone Ranger didn't

fly solo; he had Tonto!

When the going gets tough, we need _____ in

our lives we can cry out to and say, "I am in a battle, I need help! Will you

_____ with me?"

Like a wounded soldier needs his band of brothers to hoist him on

their shoulders and carry him to safety, we need men to carry us spiritu-

ally when we are too _____ or _____ to

make it through the battle on our own.

Our band of brothers are also there to give us _____

and _____ as we go through our daily lives. We

need men around us to teach us. Older saints can help the younger

saints.

A band of brothers can help each other by saying, "I _____

with this area, I _____ this going through

it, now here is how you _____ making the same

mistake."

Why should younger men have to _____ and _____ when we have gone through the same thing?

GROUP STUDY QUESTIONS

1. "No man is an island." What does this statement mean to you?

2. Does the thought of having men in your life who can ask you anything or hold you accountable freak you out? Why?

3. Why is it important for you to have an older man invest in you?

4. Who is someone older who has invested in your life?

5. How has his investment benefited your life?

6. Do you invest yourself in the life of a younger man?

7. Who is a younger guy you could invest in?

SMALL GROUP ·6· WORKBOOK

The only way to get rid of a weed is to bend down, grab it, and

_____ it out of the ground, roots and all.

The number one issue men struggle with is _____.

If we are to be men of God who are daily putting on manhood,

we need to get to the _____ of our rage, and

_____ it out once and for all.

Rage is just out of control _____ and

_____. It is the result of anger issues we al-

lowed to develop in our lives

The root of almost all anger, hate, and rage is _____.

It is time God's men stop living in this childish behavior and

start putting on manhood! We do this by once and for all facing the

_____ and _____ in our

lives and allowing the Holy Spirit to heal us.

Forgiveness is not an _____. It is a mental

_____ you need to make.

Ways to help us forgive:

I. Begin to ask God to _____ the person you

need to forgive.

2. Do something _____ for the person because Jesus taught us to do _____ to those who hate us (Luke 6:27).

3. Realize you need to forgive the person; however, forgiveness doesn't _____ their _____

_____.

True forgiveness allows you to take a stand against the evil behavior while not allowing anger, bitterness and hate to _____ you.

4. Get help from a counselor who can _____

_____.

GROUP STUDY QUESTIONS

1. Do you ever struggle with uncontrollable anger or rage?

2. What sets you off?

3. Have you been weed whacking your weeds of rage to make them look good instead of getting to the root?

4. What is keeping you from getting to the root?

5. Who are you holding unforgiveness toward?

6. This chapter suggests praying for the person you are unforgiving toward, doing something good for them, and forgiving without condoning the behavior. Which of these is hardest for you to do?

7. What can we as a group do to help you deal with your root of unforgiveness?

SMALL GROUP ▪7▪ WORKBOOK

A man who is looking to put on manhood needs to learn to live a
_____ -led life.

The Holy Spirit is the third member of the Godhead or _____
_____.

The same Holy Spirit who was present at creation, worked throughout the Old Testament, filled Jesus, and anointed and guided the early church wants to be equally active in _____
_____ today.

1. The Holy Spirit _____ us of sin.

2. The Holy Spirit _____ us into all _____
_____.

3. The Holy Spirit _____ us. This is com-
monly known as being _____ with the Holy Spirit. The initial
physical evidence, or the receipt giving us confirmation, is speaking in
_____.

4. The Holy Spirit _____ believers.

As Christians, our number one goal in life should be
_____ and _____ in
God's will for our lives.

Our heart's desire needs to be a desire to experience the

_____ that comes from living in the

Holy Spirit's truth!

The same Holy Spirit that raised Christ from the dead dwells in you (Romans 8:11)! He wants you to live the same dynamic, Spirit-filled life as the believers in _____ times.

GROUP STUDY QUESTIONS

1. What is something you learned about the Holy Spirit that you didn't know before?

2. Have there been times in your life where you ignored the direction of the Holy Spirit? What was the result?

3. In what ways has the Holy Spirit convicted you of sin in your life?

4. How does the Holy Spirit aid you in your Bible reading?

5. Have you experienced the baptism in the Holy Spirit? Describe this experience.

6. Do you allow the Holy Spirit to guide your daily life?

7. How can we as a group help you live a Spirit-led life?

SMALL GROUP ▪8▪ WORKBOOK

Live a life worthy of the calling you have received (Ephesians 4:1).

A man who is leaving his childish ways and putting on manhood needs to be a man who is _____ responsible.

How you spend your money shows _____ _____ are.

We need to show our thanks to God for allowing us to spend his money...we do this by _____.

The Bible says that a man who doesn't tithe is a man who is _____ from God. Do we really think God is going to bless us and grow us spiritually if we are _____ from him?

The number one way to ensure we are good stewards of God's money is to live on a _____.

Rather than being restrictive and oppressive, a budget is actually _____. Knowing there is enough money to pay all the bills when they are due releases enormous money _____ _____.

It's the _____ in our souls that cause us to spend money rather than save it.

PUTTING ON MANHOOD

An _____ is a craving of the soul that has never been satisfied. It is striving after or toward something.

GROUP STUDY QUESTIONS

1. Why is financial responsibility vital to putting on manhood?

2. Do you tithe? If so, why? If not, why not?

3. What does it mean to be a good steward of the remaining ninety percent?

4. What are some reasons for living on a budget? Do you live on a budget?

5. How do our appetites affect our finances?

6. What is an appetite you have to guard against in order to handle money like a godly man?

7. How can we as a group help you apply the lessons in this chapter?

SMALL GROUP •9• WORKBOOK

In order to put on manhood, a man of God needs to act like a

_____ and not a _____ with wom-

en!

    1. We need to _____ women, not _____

them.

    2. We must treat women with _____, not _____

_____.

    3. We must value a woman's _____ and _____.

    4. We need to express _____ and

_____ to women.

We as men can no longer take for granted the women in our lives.
We must let them know how grateful we are to them. We must even
pitch in and help them and make their lives easier. To fail to do this is sin.

    5. We need to see women as _____, not

_____, beings.

We are all guilty of heinous sin when we view women as sexual objects. We must change our thought patterns and mindsets so we put on
manhood.

We must retrain or reprogram our brains. The number one
way to do this is to aggressively _____ the

_____ of _____.

The second way to go about renewing our minds is through

_____. We need to spend time daily _____ to

God.

The third step to renew our mind is to eliminate the _____

from our lives.

GROUP STUDY QUESTIONS

1. Is sexual sin a sin of the mind, a sin of the eyes, or both? Explain your answer.

2. Do you struggle with trusting women or allowing yourself to rely on women?

3. Point two stated, "we need to treat women with dignity, not disgrace." What does this mean to you?

4. Do you ever struggle to let women give you wisdom and guidance? Do you think you know more than them? What is usually the result of this mindset?

5. How often do you express gratitude to the women in your life?

6. This chapter discussed treating women as spiritual, not sexual, beings and listed questions of what a man's thoughts are about when he sees something sexual. What jumped out or convicted you the most in that list?

7. Which of the five points discussed in this chapter do you struggle with the most?

8. What can we, as a group, do to help you in this area?

9. Will we as a group commit to take the one-month challenge to give up all TV and movies and replace this time with prayer and Bible reading?

SMALL GROUP ▪ 10 ▪ WORKBOOK

One of the misconceptions keeping God's men in their childish ways and from putting on manhood is that our _____ in Christ gives us _____ to do anything we want because we are no longer under the law.

Paul understood freedom in Christ doesn't give us freedom to _____ with sin; it gives us freedom to _____ sin and pursue a life of _____.

Freedom in Christ is freedom from sin's control. Christian freedom is freedom _____ sin, not freedom _____ sin.

Paul would be appalled at those who say it is okay to sin because of freedom in Christ! He knew the _____ of Christianity! He didn't take numerous floggings, stoning, imprisonment, and persecution to have the right to sin!

God requires one thing of his sons. _____!

We show our love for God when we _____ his commandments found in the Bible and stop _____ the ways of the world.

_____ is a big theological word that means every day we allow the Holy Spirit to point out areas of sin for us to face and deal with so we can change and become more like Jesus.

GROUP STUDY QUESTIONS

1. What do think the phrase freedom in Christ means?

2. Do believers have the freedom to do whatever they want whenever they want?

3. This chapter gave some examples of disputable matters. What are some areas you think are disputable matters? What are areas that are not disputable?

4. How does obedience coexist with our freedom in Christ?

5. We discussed sanctification and daily becoming more Christ-like. How do you see this happening in your life?

6. How can we as a group help you walk in obedience?

SMALL GROUP •11• WORKBOOK

"A real man of God does what needs to be done, especially when he is the last person in the world who should have to do it. Why? Because he has a servant's heart."

The simple truth of the matter is this: God never called anyone to be a _____. He only calls people to _____

_____.

God wants men with the heart of Jesus who realize no job, no task, no responsibility, nothing is _____ them. God wants men who lay down their lives with a heart of _____ to him.

Who are we to serve?

1. We are to serve _____.

2. We are to serve our _____.

3. We are to serve our _____.

God wants us to serve other _____. He wants us investing our _____ into others to help them grow in their walk with God.

GROUP STUDY QUESTIONS

1. How did Jesus model being a servant to us? What are some examples from the Bible?

2. How can you serve the unsaved to help them become believers?

3. What are some practical ways you can serve your wife?

4. How can you have a servant's heart toward your parents? What emotions does this question evoke inside of you?

5. How do you serve your children without spoiling them?

6. How can you serve your church? What skills do you have that you can use to serve?

7. How can we as a group help you develop a servant's heart?

SMALL GROUP ·12· WORKBOOK

There is nothing _____ **fears more than men who are working on laying aside their sins and breaking free of their bondages!** He **hates** when a man realizes his potential in God and grows into a strong man of God who walks in spiritual maturity. He knows such a man can't be _____!

In order to put on manhood, we have to learn to be men who _____ _____.

A man of God needs to be a man who is willing to sacrifice his _____, his _____, his _____, and his _____ wishes in order to serve others.

The thrust of the message of putting on manhood is _____ _____.

A _____ involves giving up something valuable and important to you for somebody or something you consider to be of more _____ or _____.

A man who has a heart that is willing to sacrifice _____ and _____ is a man Satan fears. Why? Because he knows he is a man who means business.

GROUP STUDY QUESTIONS

1. Why is sacrifice such a big part of putting on manhood?

2. What are some areas you could sacrifice to develop a deeper walk with God?

3. What can you sacrifice to spend more time with your family?

4. What is something you could never imagine sacrificing? What if God asked you to sacrifice this area?

5. How can we as a group help you develop a sacrificing heart?

6. Are you committed to daily putting on manhood?

Jamie Holden can be contacted at Jamie@mantourministries.com.
Feel free to send any questions, comments,
or requests for speaking engagements.

Jamie loves to speak to men and is available to speak at your next men's event. Jamie combines humor and his personal testimony to both engage and challenge men to grow in their walk with God. He uses his testimony of overcoming abuse as well as dealing with his physical and emotional issues growing up to encourage men that no matter what their background or where they have come from in life, they can grow into mighty men in God's kingdom.

"Years ago, while I was attending the University of Valley Forge, God gave me a deep desire to minister to men. My calling is to help men learn what it means to be a godly man and how to develop a deep, personal relationship with their heavenly Father. We strive to challenge and encourage men to reach their full potential in God's kingdom."

If you are interested in having Jamie at your next men's event as a speaker or workshop leader, or if you are interested in having him come share with your church, e-mail him at jamie@mantourministries.com. He is also available to speak for one or multiple weeks on the theme of his books, Putting On Manhood, Legacy: Living a Life that Lasts, and Get in the Game.

I'd love to share at your men's group!

As your planning your men's ministry calendar, connect with me to set up a time to come and share with your men!

Jamie Holden
AG US Missionary Assoc. Church Planters and Developers
Contact me at: jamie@mantourministries.com

Made in the USA
Middletown, DE
11 January 2020